ICEWINE

LUXURY BEGINS AT...... -10°C

Ask any foreigner if they know the name of a Canadian winery.
In a heartbeat they will answer "Inniskillin."

Tony Aspler

ICEWINE

DR. DONALD ZIRALDO ▪ DR. KARL KAISER

FOREWORD BY
HUGH JOHNSON

ORIGINAL DESIGN CONCEPT
MAXIMILIAN KAISER

EXTREME WINEMAKING

KEY PORTER ✒ BOOKS

Library and Archives Canada Cataloguing in Publication

Ziraldo, Donald J. P
    Icewine : extreme winemaking / Donald Ziraldo.

ISBN 978-1-55263-926-9

    1. Inniskillin Wines Inc. 2. Wine and wine making—Ontario—Niagara-on-the-Lake.
I. Title.

TP559.C3Z58 2007   663'.200971338   C2007-901830-0

THE CANADA COUNCIL | LE CONSEIL DES ARTS
FOR THE ARTS | DU CANADA
SINCE 1957 | DEPUIS 1957

ONTARIO ARTS COUNCIL
CONSEIL DES ARTS DE L'ONTARIO

The publisher gratefully acknowledges the support of the Canada Council for the Arts and the Ontario Arts Council for its publishing program. We acknowledge the support of the Government of Ontario through the Ontario Media Development Corporation's Ontario Book Initiative.

We acknowledge the financial support of the Government of Canada through the Book Publishing Industry Development Program (BPIDP) for our publishing activities.

Key Porter Books Limited
Six Adelaide Street East, Tenth Floor
Toronto, Ontario
Canada M5C 1H6

www.keyporter.com

Cover design: Catherine Didulka
Design: Counterpunch

Printed and bound in Canada

07 08 09 10 11 6 5 4 3 2 1

To all the great Canadian vintners, past, present, and future,
who have toiled in our quest for international recognition and
to the young growers and winemakers who aspire to do so in the future.

Contents

Foreword

Each of the world's classic wine regions has a distinctive identity of place. It can be as obvious as the Médoc, a long tongue of gravel and sand lapped by the Atlantic on one side and a broad river estuary on the other, or as subtle as the Côte d'Or, which on first sight seems interchangeable with a score of other hillsides in eastern France. However, when you get to know them well, their terroir—the sum of climate, soils, and terrain that stamps their personality—becomes almost tangible; their style of wine somehow an inevitable product.

The vineyards of the Niagara Peninsula come into the "obvious" category. How could any territory be more clearly defined by nature than this lake-locked, escarpment-sheltered stretch of country? Its success as a fruit garden has long been well-established. But until the 1970s it waited for its discoverers to realize it as wine country; the modern Canadian equivalent of the eager monks who created Burgundy.

Then suddenly it happened. Old fears and prejudices about the kinds of vines that could survive in Canada were tossed aside. The formidable know-how that has been accumulating in new wine districts round the world provided answers to problems that had seemed insuperable. The 1980s saw Ontario take its place at the high table of the world's cool-climate wine regions. The 1990s saw it finesse its style, identify its most privileged sites, and build its reputation beyond regional interest into the mainstream of the world's acknowledged fine wines.

Nobody will deny that in all this the Inniskillin winery has been the icebreaker. Yet the creative dedication of Donald Ziraldo reaches far beyond his own winery. As Chairman of the Vintners Quality Alliance he is shaping the ambitions of

Canada towards truly distinctive estate wines; the only route to international respect and trust.

And by the imaginative educational weapon of Inniskillin's self-guided winery tour he is teaching the new generation of Canadians to understand and appreciate the wines their country can make. This book is the logical, portable extension of the self-guided tour. It compresses, graphically and ingeniously, all the essentials of wine knowledge into an evening's study.

I salute Donald Ziraldo, his partner Karl Kaiser, and the staff at Inniskillin for another initiative that will demystify wine and bring it more friends. And I salute that ever-growing band of friends of wine and life.

Above all the 1990s saw the establishment of Icewine as the regional, and very soon national, standard bearer. How often does a whole new category join the world's wine list? Niagara has moved Icewine from a fringe benefit for ambitious vintners, occasionally achieved, to an international luxury item as dependable as it is luxurious.

Hugh Johnson, Author, *World Atlas of Wine*,
Pocket Encyclopedia of Wine, and others.

Introduction

Ice and Canada are synonymous.

The more time I spent travelling around the world introducing and promoting Icewine it became very apparent that Canada and Icewine were synonymous with each other—no small achievement when one considers that Germany created and has been making "*Eiswein*" or Icewine since 1794. Canada's recent entry into this revered world of "extreme winemaking" is very recent, and the country has become very good at it, perhaps the best. By whatever name you call it, "*Eiswein*," "Icewine," or "*Vin du Glace*," the story of this remarkable beverage begins in Germany.

We are very proud that we were able, along with our other Canadian colleagues, to take an ancient tradition from German history, interpret, and transform the making of Icewine into a Canadian icon. We can look back and marvel at the blessings that came together to create this phenomenon.

As a country once covered with glacial ice, Canada's relationship with ice is as old as time itself. The glacial sediments of the Niagara Peninsula are the result of the final phase of the Late Wisconsin glaciation (named after the state of Wisconsin where it stopped). As many as seven separate major glacial advances and retreats have occurred in the area of the Niagara Peninsula. Ice carved out the five present Great Lakes from the once singular Lake Iroquois, and the topography of the Niagara Peninsula is a direct result of glacial activity. The location of the Great Lakes in Niagara, Ontario, and Lake Okanagan in British Columbia, encourages the unique climate for Canada's wine regions and the conditions that ripen the grapes in the summer, and freezes them in the extreme winter cold. These unique climates help maintain high acids in the fruit, necessary for successfully making Icewine every year.

The other factor, which cannot be ignored, is the idea of Canada as a beautiful winter wonderland. To most people around the world, Canada represents ice, snow-capped mountains, skiing, and hockey. All these things enhance the psychological concept that Canada makes the best Icewine in the world. Similarly, Old World red wines made in Italy, France, and Spain enhance our mental images of those countries, and how we think of them.

Every wine-growing region is singularly famous, as we are for Icewine: Champagne is known for its sparkling wine, Portugal for its Port, Burgundy for its Pinot Noir and Chardonnay, and Bordeaux for its singular chateaux producing the classic blends of Cabernet Sauvignon, Cabernet Franc, and Merlot.

That brings me to the co-author of this book, Karl Kaiser, the Icewine genius and a mastermind behind the Renaissance in Icewine. Every time I hear Karl speak about Icewine I learn something new, discover some detail, or some subtle twist that I had never considered. He possesses such in-depth, inherent knowledge of Icewine, and I didn't want to leave that information undocumented. I therefore asked Karl to do a special chapter on Icewine. He brought the basics from Austria where he was born, a country also known for its Icewine. Karl's graduate work in biochemistry at Brock University further gave him the expertise to "drill down" into the subtleties of Icewine, its proper harvest, the correct fermentation, and then articulate those subtleties in the manufacture of a fine product.

Another Austrian who contributed to the appreciation of Icewine was our friend Georg Riedel, a tenth-generation glass-blower, who created the Vinum Extreme Icewine glass. The serving of the wine is so fundamental that not only did we ask Georg Reidel to create this unique Icewine glass for us, we also asked him to provide material (see pages 110–114) to further explain the instrument through which we can all better appreciate the subtle characteristics of Icewine.

I also thought it important to address the often-asked question "What food goes with Icewine?" So I enlisted a number of great chefs from around the world to contribute their expression of food and wine pairing with Icewine. The response was overwhelming, but due to space restrictions in this book I felt it was best to leave such a project for someone more qualified to create an entire book on cooking with Icewine. However, since wine and food are of such interest, we have provided a chapter on Icewine and food, as well as recipes as a tribute to Inniskillin's late resident chef Izabela Kalabis.

And since wine and food are synonymous, I felt it was important to provide not only information, but also some recipes and food pairings for Icewine, especially dessert, since Icewine is technically categorized as a dessert wine—a bit of a misnomer if you've ever sipped Icewine after a delicious bit of *foie gras*. You will never call it a dessert wine again. However you choose to enjoy Icewine, I encourage you to experiment pairing it with different kinds of food.

The evolution of wines in Canada has been nothing short of phenomenal. I especially want to acknowledge the team at Inniskillin that supports the whole concept of Inniskillin Icewine being one of the world's great wines, to Karl's winemaking team, vineyard manager Gerald Klose, and our growers who ensure we have the best fruit available. As well, I want to acknowledge people like Debi Pratt who ensure the world knows what we are doing, the boutique staff that greets and services our quests, and the strength of Vincor to build a global distribution system.

Lastly, and most importantly, are the people who support us, such as the media who write about the wines, the hospitality industry which serves our wines, and the consumer who indulges in the fruits of our labour.

Additionally, I have investigated the scientific aspects of ice, ice formation, and ice crystallization in an attempt to explain this very simple yet complex phenomenon. I have added what I consider interesting observations on various aspects of ice fromations, such as snowflakes, which cover the vineyard during the season, icebergs, ice cubes, and simply ice itself. After all, the fascination with ice is the basis for an iconic Canadian pastime: ice hockey. I also attempted to clarify the distinction between spring and fall "frost," and "freezing" in December/January, which actually makes Icewine.

We have prided ourselves in supporting Brock University's Cool Climate Oenology and Viticulture Institute (CCOVI). In recognition of our commitment, the facility is named Inniskillin Hall. I chaired the capital campaign for Niagara Culinary Institute and chaired the Vineland Research and Innovation Centre. We are very proud to share in the success and evolution of Canada as one of the rising stars in the quiet revolution of New World wines, all in the interest of education and research for future generations.

Joining that Canadian wine revolution is a number of other Canadian personalities, each well established in their area of talent. The following have announced plans to build wineries in Niagara: Mike Weir (golf), Dan Ackroyd (film and television), Wayne Gretsky (hockey), and two other friends who often write about their passion for wine, music legends Jim Cuddy (Blue Rodeo) and Stephen Page (Bare Naked Ladies), both of whom have been "Celebrity Icewine pickers."

We thank you sincerely for the support and enthusiasm which has inspired us to achieve the successes thus afforded us and the opportunity to create this book in celebration of Icewine.

So having said all that I hope you enjoy the information that we provide you with on the following pages—be cool!

Donald
www.ziraldo.ca
donald@ziraldo.ca

Icewine: The Complete Story
John Schreiner

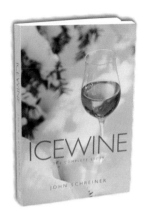

No one has done more to turn icewine into Canada's signature wine than Karl Kaiser. The talented winemaker was one of the two founding partners in 1974 of Inniskillin Wines, an elegant estate downstream from Niagara Falls and today the producer of about 100, 000 cases of some of Canada's best wines.

Kaiser's 1989 icewine established the first international credibility for Canadian icewine in 1991 when it won the illustrious Grand Prix d'Honneur at Bordeaux's Vinexpo wine fair. Almost immediately, most of Inniskillin's peers in Canada also began producing icewine, with the larger wineries, Inniskillin included, aggressively developing markets in Asia where Canadian wine previously had been unknown.

As the success of Canadian icewine rippled through the international wine world in the final decade of the twentieth century, many European wineries—some who had been occasional makers of Eiswein and some who had never made it—also joined a throng of icewine producers around the world. It is not all Karl Kaiser's doing, but he certainly played a role in starting the icewine avalanche.

Born in Austria in 1941, Kaiser intended to be a teacher. He experienced vineyard work while in the novitiate of a Cistercian monastery there and later, while helping in a vineyard owned by the grandfather of his future wife. He immigrated to Canada in 1969, planning to teach science after earning a chemistry degree and doing post-graduate work in microbiology. It was a choice of studies that equipped him well when his career switched to winemaking.

Kaiser arrived in Canada with a European wine palate and, dismayed at the sweet, foxy Canadian table wines, he planted a small home vineyard. While buying vines in 1971 at a nursery run by the Ziraldo family, Kaiser loudly disparaged

Ontario wine as unpalatable. The combative Donald Ziraldo, a University of Guelph agriculture graduate seven years younger than Kaiser, loyally defended domestic wines. Kaiser made his point by returning with a well-made bottle of his home-vintaged Chelois rosé. Ziraldo conceded that better wines could be made in Ontario and proposed that he and Kaiser should make them.

The cottage winery they opened in 1975 was the first winery licensed in Ontario in nearly 50 years. Its success inspired a wave of estate producers in all Canadian wine regions and the quality of Canadian wine began improving.

In the 1970s, the avuncular Kaiser was one of the best-trained professionals among the German-speaking winemakers in Ontario. The other transplanted wine-growers from Austria and Germany gathered often at his well-equipped Inniskillin laboratory to share ideas and ambitions. In the summer of 1983, over several bottles of wine uncorked by the ever-hospitable Kaiser, the conversation turned to icew-ine. Kaiser and Ewald Reif, a German-born grower who owned a vineyard adjacent to Inniskillin, agreed to set aside vines for icewine. So did the Austrian winemakers then working at the nearby Hillebrand Estate winery and at the Pelee Island winery in southwestern Ontario.

Only Pelee Island and Hillebrand were able to save some grapes from the birds to make small icewine vintages in 1983. All deployed nets the following year. Kaiser, who made about 900 bottles (375 ml half bottles) in 1984, ultimately outdistanced his friends. By the vintage of 1998, he made or supervised the production of about 360, 000 half bottles of icewine, undoubtedly a global record for any single wine-maker.

Kaiser's seminal contribution has not been the volume he has made but the qual-ity. His 1984 icewine—the label reads "EISWEIN Vidal (ICE WINE)" and it retailed for $18.50 when released on December 1, 1985—was the only Canadian wine to win a gold medal at the 1986 InterVin International competition in Toronto. The Grand Prix in Bordeaux five years later, the first truly significant international medal won by any Canadian winery, firmly established Inniskillin's reputation.

Kaiser used the French hybrid, Vidal, for icewine, largely because it was grown in Inniskillin's Brae Burn vineyard adjacent to the winery. "It wasn't totally a coin-cidence," he adds, "because I considered the Vidal would have the right properties. It is fruity. It has a tough skin and hangs on well to the vines. It has relatively decent acidity." He considered several other varieties, including Seyval Blanc, which also were grown nearby, but none offered Vidal's perfect package. Over time Kaiser has refined his view of what the ideal icewine grape must possess.

"It has to be aromatic because a sweet wine with no aromatic overtones is plain sugar water," he says. "It has to be late ripening. It has to have relatively high acidity and it has to have physiological properties to be durable against disease."

Besides Riesling and Vidal among the white varieties, Kaiser also has embraced Chenin Blanc, a fruity, aromatic variety "with the skin and stem of a tank." When Inniskillin established a second Canadian winery in the Okanagan Valley in 1994, Kaiser obtained Chenin Blanc for the 1994 and 1995 vintages for icewine. The variety was planted in Niagara and in 1998 Kaiser made a Chenin Blanc icewine there as well. Inniskillin Okanagan, where the winemaker is Hungarian-born Sandor Mayer, also made Ehrenfelser icewine in 1996 and, in every vintage from 1996 through 2000, has made both Vidal and Riesling icewines.

At first, Kaiser took advantage of the frigid Canadian winters to make spectacularly big wines. His 1986 Vidal icewine was made from grapes that were deeply frozen to −17°C (1°F) when pressed and the juice was 55° Brix, a honey-like sweetness. Kaiser concluded that the practical limit is −14°C (7°F); below that, the berries are so solidly frozen that the juice yield is minimal and the excessively sweet must is almost impossible to ferment. In the bitterly cold vintage of December 1996, the grapes again were picked at −17°C (1°F) and Kaiser broke two presses at Inniskillin in a near-futile effort to extract juice. "We had to wait until it was −14°C (7°F) before we saw juice coming from the press," he says. He now prefers a picking temperature of about −11°C (12°F) because it yields juice with 42° to 45° Brix, quite enough to make an icewine more sumptuously rich than many Eisweine. (For details on Brix, see "Harvesting" below.)

The longevity of his Vidal icewines has delighted him. The 1986 "is one of the ones that is holding up amazingly," Kaiser said in 1999. "There is almost no sign of oxidation. I don't know how long Vidal lives. Our 1984 is still clean as a whistle." He observes that Vidal, with a natural acidity lower than Riesling, takes on the golden hue of a mature wine earlier than Riesling.

Some Ontario winemakers, notably the Schmidt brothers at Vineland Estates, occasionally blend as much as 15 percent Riesling into the Vidal must to brighten the acidity of the finished wine without changing its lush varietal character.

"That would make sense," Kaiser agrees. "The Riesling has a more steely acid and would give a slightly firmer structure. You can blend Riesling into Vidal but not Vidal into Riesling."

The broad flavours and aroma of Vidal overwhelm Riesling's delicacy. Many Vidal icewines owe their voluptuous flavours to the effect of a typical Ontario winter, with its succession of mild freezes and thaws before the hard freeze. The Vidal grapes on the vines turn bronze and become sweeter and richer in flavour. This causes caramel and maple flavours in Ontario icewines, dramatically differentiating their style from those of Europe.

While the homespun Kaiser honed the technique of making icewine, it was his partner, Donald Ziraldo, who sold them. A daredevil extreme skier in his free time, the suave Ziraldo is the silken salesman who gets both Inniskillin and Canadian wine in front of the world's most powerful palates. In 1998, to give a characteristic example, because he was pursing Asia's icewine market, he arranged to be invited to a private reception that Canada's prime minister had in Toronto for the visiting Chinese head of state.

To give another example, Ziraldo enlisted Georg Riedel, the brilliant Austrian creator of fine crystal wine glasses, to design the "perfect" glass for icewine. Riedel has made a career of producing elegant stemware tailored to improve the sensuous enjoyment of wines. Ziraldo arranged that the preliminary trials of existing Riedel shapes be done at a tasting with some of the world's most influential wine writers, yielding a fine harvest of publicity. The long-stemmed Riedel icewine glass, with a bowl like a just-opening tulip blossom, was launched in 2000.

Ziraldo, who has received the Order of Canada, one of his nation's highest awards for achievement, made his first trip to Vinexpo in 1989. This Bordeaux exposition, properly known as Le Salon Mondial du Vin et Des Spiriteux, has become the most important of the international wine fairs. In Ziraldo's luggage were samples of Inniskillin's 1987 Vidal icewine, another powerhouse almost as concentrated as the previous vintage.

"We didn't have our own booth and there was no other Canadian winery there," Kaiser recalls. But Ziraldo, with his easy talent for mixing with the rich and famous, found influential people to taste the icewine, including an individual who identified himself as a personal friend of Jean Vidal, the breeder of the grape. "He said, when he sat down and tasted the icewine, that he would rate the wine among the five best sweet wines in the world," Kaiser recounts. This extravagant compliment spurred Ziraldo to enter an icewine at the 1991 Vinexpo.

At Kaiser's suggestion, Ziraldo took the 1989 Vidal. It was not nearly as voluptuously sweet as the previous vintages, with only about 160 grams of unfermented sugar, but with a hint of botrytis, it possessed more finesse and complexity. "It is very unusual for Vidal to get botrytis because it has a tough skin," Kaiser says. "But we had this warm Indian summer, with fog in the morning." This was ideal for the development of noble rot and the Vidal grapes had a 10 to 15 percent infection. Kaiser had been pleased with that wine from the beginning and believed it was Inniskillin's best shot at winning a medal.

As it happened, Kaiser, ever the scientist, went instead to a technical conference in Seattle rather than Vinexpo, sending his daughter Andrea to Bordeaux with the Inniskillin delegation. She called from France with the stunning news that Inniskillin had won not only one of just seventeen gold medals but what she termed "the big medal." Her mother, Sylvia, thought it was more like "the Academy Award." The publicity sent Inniskillin's icewine sales rocketing.

Inniskillin has been aggressive at introducing its wines to markets outside Canada, notably Asia. This market came to Inniskillin, as well as other wineries in the peninsula near Niagara Falls. This spectacular natural wonder is a priority attraction for Asian tourists (among others) who, when they fan out beyond the falls, discover wine touring.

At Inniskillin's quaint wine shop, the staff quickly noted that the icewine drew more notice than any other product; indeed, of every ten bottles of icewine sold at the shop, eight were being purchased by Japanese visitors. Very quickly, Inniskillin began attaching neck labels to the bottles, explaining icewine in Japanese. That was followed by supplying brochures in Japanese and employing Japanese-speaking staff to deal with the almost insatiable demand for bottles of icewine, a product ideally in tune both with the Japanese palate and with the Japanese tradition of giving each other prestige gifts.

Ever the silken salesman, Donald Ziraldo made the first of his numerous sales trips to Asia in 1997, introducing Inniskillin's 1996 icewine in Hong Kong, Singapore, and Beijing as well as Japan. In parallel with that, Inniskillin has begun its own team marketing its icewine in the United States. As European trade restrictions are lifted, Inniskillin icewines will be available there as well, including one of the few sparkling icewines in the world, created in 1999 for the Millennium.

ART

Cool-Climate Viticulture

Canada's Niagara Peninsula in Ontario and Okanagan Valley in British Columbia are considered cool-climate viticulture regions, as are Burgundy, Germany, Austria, Oregon, and New Zealand. These regions are ideally suited for the growing of Chardonnay, Pinot Noir, and Riesling. Wines from cooler climates are characteristically highly aromatic and high in acids. Their higher acidity results in wines with longer natural aging potential. Winemakers believe that cool climates produce lighter, fruitier wines, whereas hotter regions produce less fruity, heavier wines.

The Niagara Peninsula is located on the 43rd latitude, the same as northern California and more southerly than Burgundy, while the Okanagan Valley is located on the 49th latitude.

Pinot Noir was grown in the cool-climate viticulture regions of Burgundy as early as the first century B.C. The first vineyards were established by the Romans, although it is believed that the Gauls had domesticated some wild vines for winemaking long before the Romans arrived. It is also thought that the Pinot Noir grape is indigenous to Burgundy. Its resistance to winter frost is a characteristic of the grape. Quality Pinot Noir is best achieved under cool-climate conditions such as those of the Niagara Peninsula; in warmer climates Pinot Noir loses its elegance and finesse. A slow maturing process seems to be a prerequisite for the development of delicate aromas and freshness. Nevertheless, microclimatic differences influence the behaviour of Pinot Noir, and the broad variation that can be found from vintage to vintage is an expression of that sensitivity. A good example is Pinot Noir in California, where it best expresses its characteristics in the cooler Carneros region of Napa and Sonoma.

Chardonnay, on the other hand, is much more adaptable across a wide range of climatic conditions and can exhibit vastly different personalities. In warm climates such as Australia it tends to exhibit ripe, dense fruit flavours such as pineapple and mango paired with low acidity. Chardonnays from cool climates are characterized by their delicacy, finesse, and firm acidity with subtle flavours of apple and grapefruit.

In general, cooler continental climates such as the Niagara Peninsula and the Okanagan Valley are subject to greater extremes—that is, hotter summers and cooler winters—than the warmer regions of Europe and California, resulting in considerable variability between vintages. Vintage charts from cool-climate regions such as Burgundy show much more variability than do most vintage charts from hot climates such as Italy and Australia.

Cold winter temperatures are a significant limiting factor in viticulture. Winter injury to the vine can be quite common and bud damage can occur if the temperature falls below –20°C (–4°F). In North America, commercial viticulture is confined

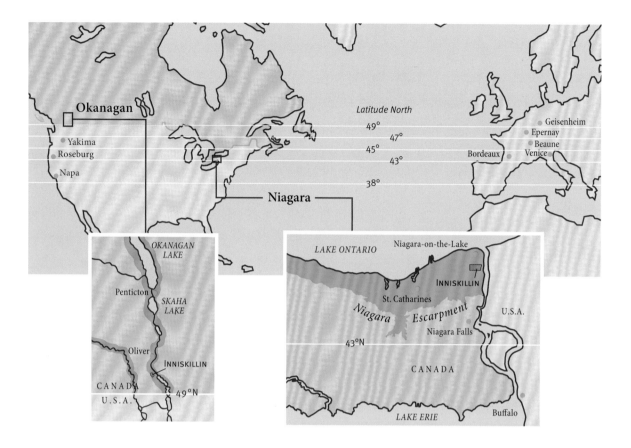

Top: Latitude comparison between North America and Europe; bottom left, Okanagan Valley, BC; bottom right, Niagara Peninsula, ON.

to southern regions such as California or water-moderated regions such as Long Island and Niagara. Continental viticultural areas in North America are exposed to not only lower mid-winter temperatures, but also greater fluctuations in temperature. This results in a greater temperature range and subsequently more variable vintages.

Fortunately, Lake Ontario, a large, deep mass of water, has a major influence on the climate in the Niagara region. The lake absorbs and stores vast amounts of heat that it releases whenever the surrounding air and land are cooler than the lake. This continuous airflow over the land surface not only moderates winter temperatures but also reduces the risk of spring frost.

Another major criterion for cool-climate definition is the rapid cooling of night temperatures during the crucial ripening months of September and October.

Northern latitudes, generally associated with cool-climate viticulture, have shorter growing seasons. As a result, the rate at which grapes accumulate sugar and lose acid is slower than in more southern regions.

Icewine is one of the most famous wines produced in cool-climate viticulture areas. It can be grown only in cool-climate conditions and owes much of its greatness to the very high level of acidity in the wine. This acidity is necessary to sustain the equilibrium between it and the tremendous concentration of sugar in the grapes, and results in a beautifully balanced wine with great finish on the palate.

The most important factor in Icewine production is low temperature during harvesting, which increases the extract, fullness, and aroma in the wine. Icewine is a high-risk wine, as yields are very low—often as little as 5 percent of the crop.

Latitude and altitude are also important indicators of climatic suitability. Both affect the amount and length of sunlight during the day and the relative coolness of nighttime temperatures. In cool-climate viticultural areas, the reduced sunlight produces high levels of odour-active compounds because of slow fruit maturation. Odour-active compounds (esters and aldehydes) are detected by the nose and are recognized as familiar smells of grape (primary) aromas. For example, the terpinol in Gewürztraminer produces a "spicy" odour.

There are several ways to measure the wine-growing potential of a region. The most common is "growing degree" days. They are measured as the sum of the monthly mean temperatures over 10°C (50°F), below which there is little, if any, physiological activity in the vines, from April 1 to October 31. The chart above shows the median growing degree days in the major cool-climate viticulture regions.

The hours of sunshine and the temperature in a region both play important roles in the growth potential of the vine. These two influences are interrelated but should not be confused. In cooler climates, temperature rather than sunshine becomes the limiting factor in determining the potential for growth. In warmer climates, temperatures are already adequate and it is the number of sunshine hours that will ultimately govern maturity.

As perennial plants, grapevines have developed mechanisms to ensure survival during seasons of unfavourable weather. However, to ensure long-term consistent production and maintain the required quality of fruit in cooler climates, humans have become part of the survival mechanism through vineyard management.

There are many factors to manage for cold endurance: the grower must understand the nature of vine maturation, dormancy, canopy management, training systems,

GROWING DEGREE DAYS MEASURED IN CELSIUS

Geisenheim, Germany	1050
Epernay, France (Champagne)	1050
Hawke's Bay, New Zealand	1200
Roseburg, Oregon	1250
Geneva, Switzerland	1250
Beaune, France (Burgundy)	1315
Niagara, Canada	1426
Oliver, British Columbia	1423
Yakima, Washington	1426
Napa, California	1450
Healsburg, Sonoma, California	1755

The sum of the monthly mean temperatures over 10°C (50°F) from April 1 to October 31.

rootstocks, water and soil management, nutrient requirements, and clonal selection. Clones are selected from a large population of grapevines. Clones exhibit superior characteristics and function to achieve specific and unique quality and to eliminate viruses. Clonal selection has played a large role in the development of cultivars specific to cool-climate growing conditions by enabling the grower to select characteristics that may have a significant impact on the quality of the finished wine.

A wine region's soil structure greatly determines the heat retention and water-holding capacity of the soil. Because it influences the vine's performance, the soil's structure is considered to be even more important than its chemical composition.

Although climate may be the determining factor in deciding where to plant grapes and which grape varieties to plant—for example, Pinot Noir in Niagara vs. Merlot in the Okanagan Valley—the "terroir" will continue to be debated as the great contributor to the art of wine.

Climate

As mentioned above, the Niagara Peninsula is located at 43°N, placing it in the same latitude as Northern California and more southerly than Burgundy, which is at 47°N, as illustrated (page 24). With an average annual heat summation of 1426 growing-degree days (see page 25) the Niagara Peninsula falls into the category of cool climate.

The Niagara Region is ideal for making Icewine due to its maritime influence and continental climate. Annual rainfall is approximately 700 to 800 mm, although unpredictable September and October rains occur. Grapevine flowering generally occurs from about June 10 to 18.

The moderating effect of Lake Ontario is illustrated on page 27. With the Niagara Escarpment, the lake creates a unique microclimate that allows for the growing of Vitis vinifera.

Using a comparison based upon growing-degree days (the summation of all degrees accumulated over 10°C during the potential growing season from April 1 to October 31), the Niagara Peninsula compares favourably with some of the finest cool grape-growing areas.

GRAPE CLIMATIC ZONES IN NIAGARA

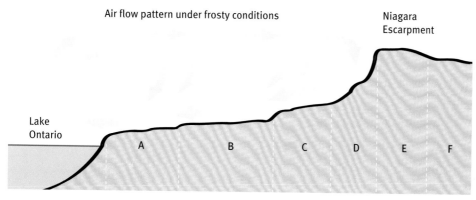

Air flow pattern under frosty conditions

Niagara
Escarpment

Lake
Ontario

A   B   C   D   E   F

A   Lakeshore effect zone
B   Level plain between escarpment and lake
C   Base of escarpment slope plus steep slope east of St. Catharines
D   Steep north-facing escarpment slopes
E   Slopes above the escarpment
F   Flat and rolling land south of the escarpment

MONTHLY AVERAGE TEMPERATURE °C

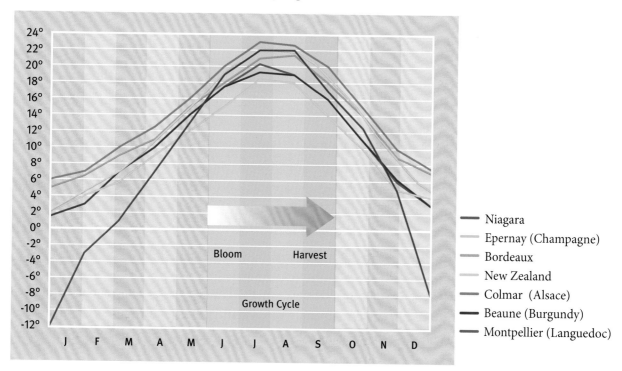

— Niagara
— Epernay (Champagne)
— Bordeaux
— New Zealand
— Colmar (Alsace)
— Beaune (Burgundy)
— Montpellier (Languedoc)

Bloom   Harvest

Growth Cycle

The most critical aspect of the growth cycle, as shown on the chart (page 27, bottom) is that growth between bloom (June 10–18) and harvest (October–November) is approximately the same as other wine regions throughout the world, 100–112 days.

Due to its unique geographic location between the Great Lakes and the interior of the North American continent, in this critical period Niagara is warmer than regions such as Alsace and Champagne. This chart (page 27) also illustrates that the cold winter temperatures in Niagara, which allow for the production of Icewine in December and January, generally will not affect the vines because they are in their dormant state. They do, however, provide the temperature plunges that crystallize the water in the fruit to create authentic Icewine.

Soil and Geography

NIAGARA

Soil is a critical element in viticulture. The physiology and geology of the Niagara Peninsula both affect the growing of grapes.

The Niagara Peninsula (see map below) is a distinct geological region in Southern Ontario. It is bound on the north by Lake Ontario, the south by Lake Erie, and the east by the Niagara River.

The backbone of the peninsula is the Niagara Escarpment, a cuesta (ridge) 30 to 50 m high. This escarpment extends along the entire Niagara Peninsula, influences the soil, and creates microclimates. North of the escarpment is a flat plain, the result of deposits of lacustrine clays, sands, and gravel on the bottom of the old Lake Iroquois. Lake Iroquois was a single lake that existed before the last Ice Age; from it developed the existing five Great Lakes. In some places the soil is modified by river valley alluvium, mostly sand and gravel. It is only this area, below the escarpment and on the first bench (one of the levels on the escarpment), that favours the growing of premium grapes.

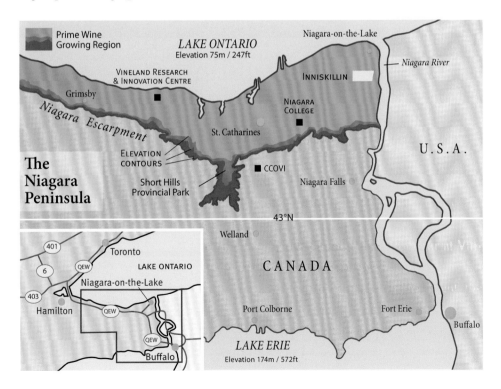

Niagara Peninsula, located between Lake Ontario and Lake Erie, which is within the permanent Greenbelt.

The bedrock of the escarpment contains siliceous sandstones, ferruginous sandstones, limestones, and dolomites of Devonian age. Since the escarpment was at one time the shoreline of Lake Iroquois, the deposited soil comprises many different types (clay, clay-loam, loam, sand, etc.). Soil is generally deep and includes a considerable quantity of mineral material from the different types of bedrock, ultimately influencing the nutrition of the vineyards.

ANATOMY OF THE NIAGARA ESCARPMENT
AT THE CANADIAN HORSESHOE FALLS

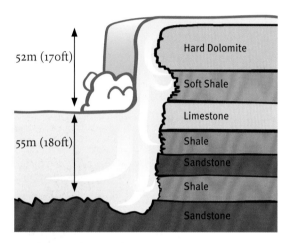

52m (170ft)

55m (180ft)

Hard Dolomite

Soft Shale

Limestone

Shale

Sandstone

Shale

Sandstone

Canadian Horseshoe Falls dropping over falls and exposed bedrock.

Face of the Niagara Escarpment with exposed bedrock at the Niagara Gorge.

SOIL TYPES IN THE NIAGARA WINE-GROWING REGION
Cross-section of the Niagara Peninsula

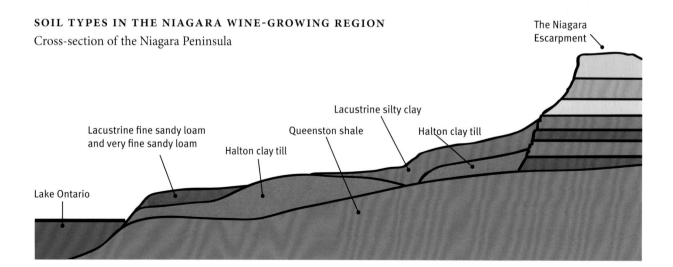

The Niagara Escarpment

Lacustrine silty clay

Lacustrine fine sandy loam and very fine sandy loam

Queenston shale

Halton clay till

Halton clay till

Lake Ontario

One of the two critical elements that are responsible for the mesoclimate which allows us to grow Vitis vinifera grapes in Niagara is the Niagara Escarpment. About 12,000 years ago Niagara Falls cascaded over the face of the Niagara Escarpment at Queenston. It has since moved downstream through the gorge approximately 11 km to its present location at the Horseshoe Falls in the city of Niagara Falls. The tumbling waters, as seen in the photo above, erode the softer layers of sandstone and shale below the hard top layer of dolomite limestone, creating the 11 km–long Niagara Gorge as illustrated on the facing page (top left).

Horseshoe Falls, Niagara Falls in January.

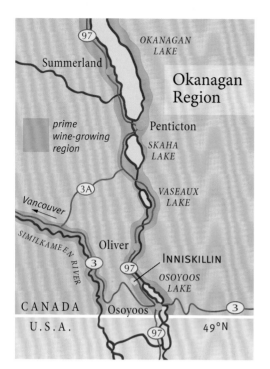

Okanagan Valley.

OKANAGAN

Inniskillin Okanagan commenced as a partnership between Inniskillin and the Inkameep Indian Band (Okanaquen Tribe) in the Okanagan Valley in British Columbia. Inniskillin established an estate winery in the Okanagan in 1994, which commemorated 20 years of Inniskillin's first crush.

The labels were designed by a local artist. Great care was taken to ensure that the labels reflected the Native heritage. The label inspired the naming of our estate vineyard: Dark Horse Vineyard.

The Okanagan Valley climatic region is much drier than Niagara and unique as a grape-growing region in Western Canada. The valley is at the same latitude as the Rhine Valley in Germany and the Champagne region of France. The region stretches for 130 km, from Lake Osoyoos, at 49°N, just north of the Canada/ U.S. border, to the northern tip of Okanagan Lake. The lakes moderate the temperatures throughout the year. Intense sunlight and minimal rainfall allow the grapes to ripen to their full maturity, while cool nights help them to retain high acidity. These climatic conditions, along with a unique soil structure, produce wines that are full-bodied and highly flavoured with good acidity.

The climate is only one element of the larger system at play, called an ecosystem. The southern Okanagan Valley is positioned at the northernmost tip of the Sonoran Desert, starting in Mexico and extending through North America as the Great Basin, with ancient origins probably dating back 10,000 years. The Valley provides the hot, dry summers and mild winters characteristic of the arid antelope-brush ecosystem. In the warmest part of the south Okanagan Valley is a pocket of dry grassland dominated by bunchgrasses, the wind, and the scraggly dark branches of antelope-brush.

This region is ideally suited for the growing of premium Vitis vinifera grapes. Annual precipitation is about 25 cm. Moisture from precipitation travels quickly through the sandy or gravelly soils, so few plants can grow in these soils in arid areas. The low available water storage capacity of the soils therefore requires irrigation in order to grow grapevines in these otherwise desert conditions.

On the east side of the Okanagan Valley are moderately sloping terraces and benches (Osoyoos Lake Bench) that lie between the northeast side of Osoyoos Lake and the

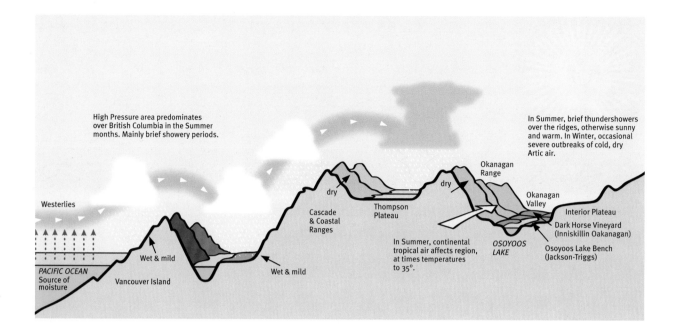

High Pressure area predominates over British Columbia in the Summer months. Mainly brief showery periods.

In Summer, brief thundershowers over the ridges, otherwise sunny and warm. In Winter, occasional severe outbreaks of cold, dry Artic air.

Westerlies

Okanagan Range

Okanagan Valley

dry

dry

Cascade & Coastal Ranges

Thompson Plateau

Interior Plateau

Dark Horse Vineyard (Inniskillin Oakanagan)

In Summer, continental tropical air affects region, at times temperatures to 35°.

OSOYOOS LAKE

Osoyoos Lake Bench (Jackson-Triggs)

Wet & mild

Vancouver Island

Wet & mild

PACIFIC OCEAN
Source of moisture

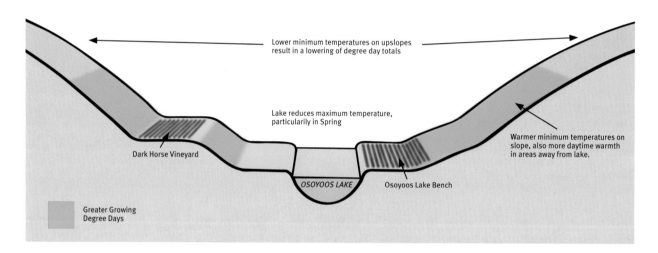

Lower minimum temperatures on upslopes result in a lowering of degree day totals

Lake reduces maximum temperature, particularily in Spring

Warmer minimum temperatures on slope, also more daytime warmth in areas away from lake.

Dark Horse Vineyard

OSOYOOS LAKE

Osoyoos Lake Bench

Greater Growing Degree Days

Cross-section of coastal range and Okanagan Valley.

steep, rocky mountain slopes to the east. Inkameep and Mica Creeks, passing westward through the area, provide the main drainage. The soil of this area is derived from wind-blown sands and gravels deposited by the meltwaters of the Ice Age glaciers.

The surficial geologic materials (soil parent materials) are dominantly sandy glaciofluvial deposits, some with gravelly subsoils. Very fine sandy and coarse silty glaciolacustrine deposits also occur in the vicinity of Inkameep Creek and proba-bly underlie portions of the sandy glaciofluvial materials at depth elsewhere. Thin, sandy veneers of eolian (windblown) material sometimes occur in areas protected from the wind. Along the extreme eastern boundary of the area, large boulders and

stones sometimes occur on, and in, the soil. These originated from the adjacent steep, rocky mountain slopes. The soils are all Brown Chernozems (as classified in the Canadian Soil Classification). They have a grayish brown surface horizon about 15 cm thick that is slightly enriched with organic matter. Under this is a moderately weathered yellowish brown to light brown zone that is about 20 cm thick and usually non-calcareous. Under this is unweathered soil parent material that is sometimes calcareous.

On the west side of the Valley, the soils underlying the Inniskillin Dark Horse Vineyard are classified as Ratnip (soil parental materials), which consist of gravelly, coarse textured fluvial fan deposits. Textures range from gravelly, sandy loam to gravelly, loamy sand. Surface stones vary from few on the fan apron to many at the fan apex—much of it from the Hester Creek fan deposits.

Icewine grapes hanging on the vine in January in Okanagan.

VQA

The Vintners Quality Alliance—vQA—is an Appellation of Origin system by which consumers can identify Canadian wines based on the origin of the grapes from which they are produced.

With the vQA system, Canada joins other leading wine-producing countries in developing a body of regulations and setting high standards for its finest wines. In 1935, for example, France introduced its Appellation d'Origine Contrôlée system, which remains in place today. Italy introduced its Denominazione d'Origine Controllata designation in 1963. Germany's Qualitatswein mit Predikat system was finalized in 1971, and the U.S. system in 1978.

In Ontario the vQA officially started in 1988. The Ontario vQA then requested that British Columbia undertake a similar system, which it did in 1990. Each region maintains unique regulations that are specific to it, just as Burgundy and Bordeaux do. All wine-growing regions in France function under the French Appellation of Origin system, governed by the Institute National Des Appellations D'Origine (INAO).

Experience has shown that certain vineyard areas, because of their favoured soils, exposure, and microclimate, produce the best wines year after year. By designating the appellations of origin on the label, vintners provide the consumer with information about the origin of the grapes, particularly the terroir in which they are grown. As in the centuries-old wine regions of Burgundy and Chianti, refinements to the existing regulations within the vQA are continually being made, such as the introduction of sub-appellations in 2005.

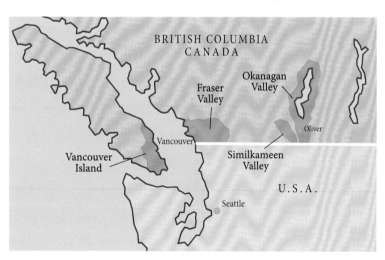

DESIGNATED VITICULTURAL AREAS IN BRITISH COLUMBIA

Okanagan Valley
Similkameen Valley
Fraser Valley
Vancouver Island

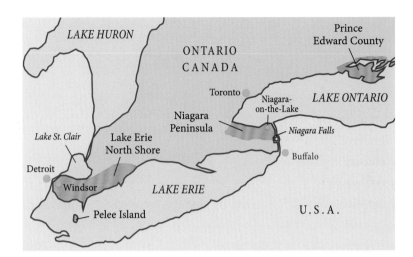

Niagara Peninsula
Pelee Island
Lake Erie North Shore
Prince Edward County

There are two distinct wine-growing regions in Canada—the provinces of Ontario and British Columbia. The VQA recognizes within Ontario three Designated Viticultural Areas (DVA): Niagara Peninsula, Pelee Island, and Lake Erie North Shore. In British Columbia, the VQA recognizes four DVA: the Okanagan Valley, the Similkameen Valley, the Fraser Valley, and Vancouver Island.

The VQA is a legislated wine authority.

A stringent code of regulations governs the right of vintners to use these highly specific geographic designations on their labels. Only Vitis vinifera varieties such as Chardonnay, Pinot Noir, and Riesling can be grown in the DVAs, and wines must be produced from 100 percent Canadian-grown grapes. For varietals, 85 percent of the wine must be made from the variety named on the label, and the wine must exhibit the predominant character of that variety. If a vintner wishes to designate the vineyard from which the wine was made, the site must be within a recognized viticultural area (DVA) and 100 percent of the grapes must come from that vineyard.

Wines are evaluated by an independent panel of experts. Only those wines that meet or exceed the production and appellation standards are awarded VQA status and are entitled to display the VQA medallion. In 2005, a wine authority was created in British Columbia to regulate the VQA.

To make Icewine in Ontario, the VQA requires that:

- The wine is produced by VQA–registered growers and winemakers.
- The alcohol is derived exclusively from the natural sugars of the grapes.
- The finished wine must have a Brix of 35° or higher, and there must be residual sugar of 125 g/l and a minimum Brix of 32° in the juice after pressing when measured in the fermentation tank.
- The harvest of Icewine grapes must start after November 15.

Before harvesting, the producer must verify in writing, (by specified form) the following:

- ❧ the temperatures of each individual harvest
- ❧ the acreage and tonnage of each given crop
- ❧ the measured Brix level of each must
- ❧ the harvesting date and time of day
- ❧ Icewine pressing capacity.

All VQA Icewine processors are required to attend a VQA Icewine Standards Seminar each year.

VQA authorities randomly sample and analyze must, juice, and wine to ensure the standards are being met. These third-party inspectors are sometimes referred to as the "Icewine police."

In 2000, Canada, Germany, and Austria signed an international agreement on the production and quality standards for Icewine to protect consumers everywhere from fake Icewines. The wine-grower associations of the three countries also agreed to promote among their respective governments and multilateral organizations these Icewine standards. These international standards cleared a major hurdle for Canadian Icewine to be marketed in Europe.

Armin Goring, Director of the Deutsches Weininstitut, Mainz, noted that "part of the charm of Icewine/Eiswein is the natural production process and the risks that it entails for the producer. The harvesting and pressing conditions contribute to its unique taste, persona, and its price given the intense nature of its production and relatively limited supply[1]."

Shortly after the signing of the agreement the United States ruled that wine made from grapes artificially frozen after the harvest may not be labelled Icewine. In 2003, the Office International de la Vigne et du Vin (OIV) based in Paris endorsed this position when it prohibited wines made from artificially frozen grapes from being called Icewine, Vin du Glace, or Eiswein.

HOW TO READ A WINE LABEL

The winery

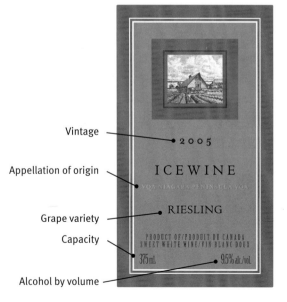

Vintage — 2005

Appellation of origin — ICEWINE
VQA NIAGARA PENINSULA VQA

Grape variety — RIESLING

Capacity — PRODUCT OF/PRODUIT DU CANADA
SWEET WHITE WINE/VIN BLANC DOUX
375 mL

Alcohol by volume — 9.5% alc./vol.

VQA NIAGARA PENINSULA SUB-APPELLATION

In December, 2005, new regulations which designate twelve sub-appellations within the grape-growing region of the Niagara Peninsula were established. The purpose of establishing sub-appellations is to fulfill VQA Ontario's role in maintaining the integrity of Ontario's wines of origin through regulations, and ensuring that claims of origin are appropriate in the interest of both consumers and VQA members. As well, VQA hopes to further educate the public about the importance of origin and terroir in terms of where the grapes are grown and promote the unique characteristics of wines produced from these sub-appellations.

Within the Niagara Peninsula, there are spatially distinctive areas or sub-appellations and each possesses a distinguishing array of physical characteristics that make it uniquely different from the others. At this smaller scale, these environmental characteristics and their distribution in space are generally recognized to influence the choice of cultivars, and most importantly, the differences in grape and wine quality and viticultural practices.

New appellations and sub-appellations continue to be defined throughout the wine world, especially in the new world regions where interest in terroir is increasing.

The new sub-appellations are: Niagara Lakeshore, Niagara River, Four Mile Creek, St. David's Bench (Niagara-on-the-Lake), Creek Shores, Lincoln Lakeshore, Beamsville Bench, Twenty Mile Bench, Short Hills Bench, and Vinemount Ridge (Niagara Escarpment).

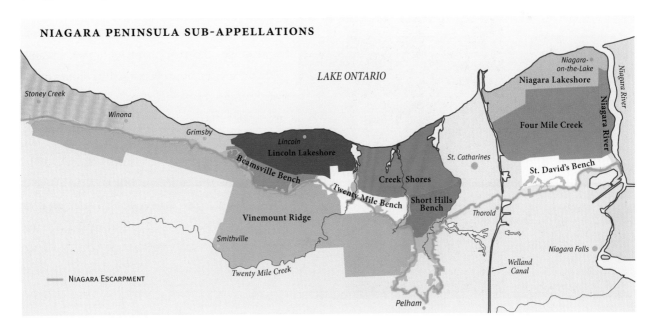

NIAGARA PENINSULA SUB-APPELLATIONS

I have selected several examples to illustrate in more detail:

Niagara River

A prominent and unique feature of this sub-appellation is the preponderance of east-facing slopes. The soils of this sub-appellation have developed on the bedrock belonging to the Queenstown Formation, a red shale with high silt and clay content. In the northern portion of this sub-appellation, approximately 18 percent of the soils are poorly-drained, silty, and clayey. The influence of the Niagara River that runs parallel to this sub-appellation is approximately 1 km wide at its widest point. The influence of Lake Ontario on the mesoclimate of this sub-appellation is felt primarily on cold, windy nights when north winds cross the warmer waters of Lake Ontario. Cool breezes from Lake Ontario may also reach the northern half of the sub-appellation on hot summer days.

Beamsville Bench

This sub-appellation slopes gradually from the base of the Niagara Escarpment northwards, marking the Lake Iroquois Shore Bluff. This stretch of the Bench has steep to moderate slopes that were cut by numerous streams during the Holocene Period (about 10,000 years ago), ready channels that eventually flowed into Lake Ontario. These short slopes of moderate gradient not only provide excellent drainage in the sub-soil, but on nights with damaging frosts, they also provide rapid, cold-air drainage. Soils in this sub-appellation range in thickness from 1 to 20 m. About 81 percent of the soils are silty, clay loams. The most striking feature of the soils is the variegated colours of red, yellow, and olive clays occuring in approximately equal proportions, reflecting the colours of the shale and sandstone bedrock.

Clos Jordenne Vineyard at sunset.

Viticulture

All grapevines originated as wild vines. Grape culture is believed to have begun in the region between and to the south of the Caspian and Black seas, where grapes were first domesticated. Asia Minor, as this region is known, is home to the Vitis vinifera, the species from which all cultivated grape varieties were derived before the discovery of North America. In the Bible, in the Book of Genesis (IX, 20), Noah was said to enjoy growing grapes and making wine. Several centuries before Christ, vines were carried to Greece, then to Rome. It was the Romans who were generally responsible for spreading vines throughout Europe.

All vines are in the botanical family Vitaceae (see chart). Grapevines are of the genera, Vitis (from Latin *viere*, meaning to twist), vines which climb by tendrils. Vitis is then separated into two sub-genera, one of which is Euvitis. The principal species of Euvitis is Vitis vinifera (meaning wine-bearing), the Old World species that produces over 90 percent of the world's grapes. Some of these species are recognized as the classic varieties, such as Cabernet Sauvignon, Cabernet Franc, Merlot, Pinot Noir, Chardonnay, Riesling, Sauvignon Blanc, and others. Grapevines were spread from region to region by mankind. This is often mentioned in the Bible. It is apparent that the grape has been a food to mankind from the earliest of times.

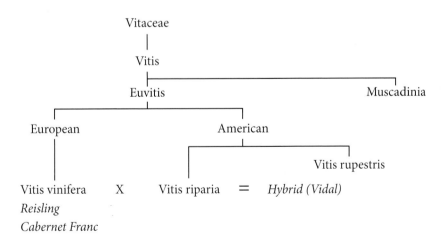

Vitis riparia and Vitus rupestris are indigenous grapevines in North America. These species are inherently resistant to phyloxera vasatrix (Daclylosphaera vitifoliae) (see story, inset), the root louse, which is also native to North America. Phyloxera is largely controlled by the use of these species as rootstocks. To prevent phyloxera infection, which is basically restricted to the soil, the Vitis vinifera species are grafted onto resistant rootstocks from the above species.

Vitis vinifera vines first appeared in North America via the Spaniards in Mexico, and were then planted in the Baja region of California in the late 1600s and in the late 1700s arrived at the Mission in San Diego. In Canada, wild vines, probably Vitis riparia, were discovered by Jacques Cartier and later by Jesuit missionaries in the 1600s along the St Lawrence River. Vitis vinifera was introduced into Canada in the 1940s and came into commercial production in the 1970s.

PHYLOXERA

When vines were first brought back to Europe from America by an adventuresome explorer in the mid 1800s, the phyloxera was a "stowaway" and soon infected the non-resistant Vitis vinifera. That epidemic almost wiped out the European wine industry in the 1860s. In Europe it was discovered that by planting the resistant rootstocks and grafting the Vitis vinifera on top of the phyloxera-resistant rootstock it would not be attacked by the soil-borne phyloxera. This practice is now common throughout the viticultural world.

LIFE OF THE VINE: GRAPEVINE PHYSIOLOGY

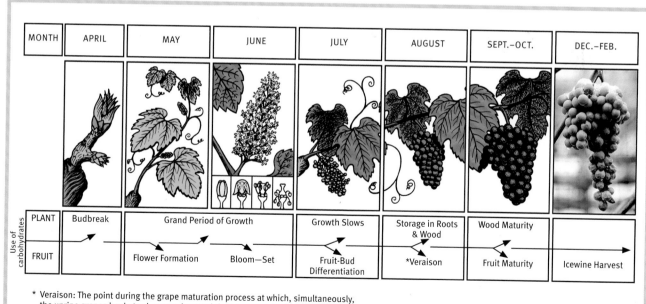

MONTH	APRIL	MAY	JUNE	JULY	AUGUST	SEPT.–OCT.	DEC.–FEB.

Use of carbohydrates

| PLANT | Budbreak | Grand Period of Growth | | Growth Slows | Storage in Roots & Wood | Wood Maturity | |
| FRUIT | | Flower Formation | Bloom—Set | Fruit-Bud Differentiation | *Veraison | Fruit Maturity | Icewine Harvest |

* Veraison: The point during the grape maturation process at which, simultaneously, the unripe grapes begin to change colour and their sugar content begins to increase.

GRAPE VARIETIES

Cabernet Franc (Cab'-air'nay Fronc)

Cabernet Franc is perhaps most famous for its contribution to the truly great wines of Saint-Emilion, Bordeaux. It is also the sole constituent of most of the finest red wines of the Loire Valley in France. Cabernet Franc Icewine generally has a slight brick red colour. This chacteristic makes it the most appropriate red variety for Icewine production. The aroma often shows hints of strawberry and rhubarb.

Riesling (Reese-ling)

This variety is often said to be to Germany what the Chardonnay is to France. Like Chardonnay, Riesling is one of the "noble" varieties, and as such its popularity has led to plantings throughout the world. Riesling, by nature, carries a fairly high acidity, particularly in cool climates, which makes it ideal for Icewine. This makes an excellent counterweight for high degrees of residual sugar in the Icewine. This natural acid backbone allows Rieslings to age gracefully and improve and develop over time.

Vidal (Vee-dahl)

Vidal 256 is an aromatic, winter-hardy, white French hybrid created by crossing Ugni Blanc (Trebianno) and one of the Seibel parents, Rayon d'Or (Seibel 4986; an interspecific cross in 1920 by Jean L. Vidal in Charante, France).

Its slow, steady ripening, thick skin, long hang time, and high aromatics make it ideal for Icewine. The tropical fruit aromas range from lychee and, mango, to dried apricots.

Varietal: A varietal wine is any wine that is distinguished by and labelled according to the grape variety from which it was made. For example, Riesling Icewine is made from the Riesling grape.

Harvesting

Once the temperature descends to –8°C (18°F) (official VQA harvest temperature) the harvest can officially begin. Although harvesting is done predominantly by hand, mechanical harvesting with sophisticated mechanical harvesters is becoming increasingly prevalent (see page 83).

The sugar content of the grapes for Icewine is directly related to the temperature and is measured with a refractometer (see page 102). The freezing process increases the Brix level in the grapes dramatically, as illustrated in the table below.

Brix, also known as degrees Brix or balling, is a measurement used to define the sweetness of grapes. Brix refers to the percentage of dissolved solids in the juice (almost all of which are sugars) and can be used by winemakers to calculate the natural potential alcohol of the wine to be made, as illustrated in the chart below. As a general rule, the natural potential alcohol is calculated by dividing Brix of the fruit at harvest by two.

CROSS-SECTION OF A RIESLING GRAPE

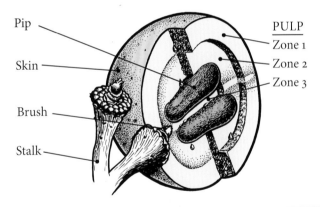

Pip
Skin
Brush
Stalk

PULP
Zone 1
Zone 2
Zone 3

MEASUREMENTS OF SUGAR CONTENT (BRIX)

	Table wine					Icewine
Specific Gravity	1.085	1.090	1.095	1.100	1.105	1.176
°Oechsle (Germany)	85	90	95	100	105	176
Baumé (France)	11.3	11.9	12.5	13.1	13.7	22.2
Brix (North America)	20.4	21.5	22.5	23.7	24.8	40
% Potential Alcohol	10.6	11.3	11.9	12.5	13.1	10% + 220 gm/l residual sugar

The table (left) shows three systems for measuring the sugar content of grapes and their relationship to the potential alcohol of the resulting wine.

Cooperage

The use of oak to store wine dates back over 2000 years. Cooperage is the craft of making barrels; the craftsman is known as the cooper. The barrel-making process for wine is also more than 2000 years old; its stages are shown in the photographs below.

The wood used is as important to the cooper as the selection of grapes is to the winemaker. Many of the most prized oaks are French (facing page): Limousin, Nevers, Troncais, Allier, and Vosges. All have varying degrees of porousness ranging from open grain to tight grain (see page 47).

Oak aging is used sparingly in the making of Icewine. Oak is used almost exclusively with Vidal to create a more complex structure for this unique Canadian varietal. Riesling, a much more subtle and delicate varietal, is traditionally made in stainless steel.

Although the cost of oak is high, many of the world's finest wines, such as Chateau d'Yquem, owe their character, complexity, and quality to aging in small oak barrels.

There are numerous variables when choosing a wine barrel. The winemaker has the opportunity to choose the cooper, wood type, forest, grain, size of barrel, and the toast. All affect the final product.

The changes that occur during the wine's aging process are enormously complex. In barrel aging the first is extraction, in which the tannins, vanilla, oak lactones, and other phenolics are extracted from the wood. The second is oxidation,

Splitting

Assembling & shaping

Firing (toasting)

in which the tannins, acids, and other components of the wine react to a gradual exposure to oxygen through the grain of the wood.

The amount and type of aging that a wine should receive are both a function of the wine qualities such as colour or tannin, and the style of wine being produced.

The use of oak aging to add complexity to Icewine is unique to some Canadian wineries. The traditional German Icewines and most Canadian Icewine is made exclusively in stainless steel to maintain the fresh fruit, youth, and character of the Icewine.

THE OAK FORESTS OF FRANCE

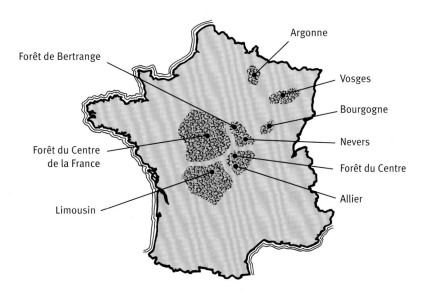

Troncais oak—tight grain

limousin oak—open grain

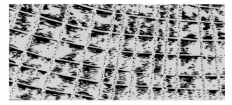

Grain	Forest	Characteristics
Open	Limousin	Limousin wood perfumes and colours the wine rapidly with little finesse.
Average	Bourgogne Nevers	Bourgogne and Nevers wood gives a vanilla flavour and balance to the wine.
Tight	Allier Troncais Vosges	The wood of Allier, Troncais and Vosges releases its perfumes slowly, with finesse.

Cork

The use of natural cork as a closure for wine bottles is a centuries-old practice. Recently there has been a significant movement toward screw caps in an attempt to eliminate "corked" wines.

Cork is obtained from the layer just beneath the bark of the cork oak tree (Quercus suber), grown most extensively in Portugal (top left), Spain, and Algeria, and to a lesser extent in other Mediterranean countries.

Cork oak trees have a life span of 300–400 years, although they seldom grow to heights of more than 12 m. Trees must be approximately 50 years of age before they produce cork suitable for wine stoppers.

Once a tree is ready for harvest, workers strip the bark in June, July, or August, using long-handled hatchets (top right). Each tree may be harvested only once every eight to ten years.

Oblong sections of bark are carefully pried off the tree using the wedge-shaped handle of the hatchet. The inner layer of cork bark will continue to produce cork as long as it has not been bruised by the stripper's hatchet.

Slabs of stripped bark are then boiled, and the tough, gritty outer layer scraped off. The boiling dissolves tannic acid from the cork and softens the slabs so they can be straightened, laid flat, and packed into bundles.

Cork bottle closures are punched out of these slabs (above left), sorted for quality, sterilized, and packaged for shipment worldwide.

Icewine

Originally developed in the 1700s in the cool-climate wine regions of Europe—Germany and Austria—the production of Icewine is ideally suited to Niagara's climatic conditions.

The grapes are left on the vine well into December and January. The ripe berries are dehydrated through the constant freezing and thawing during these winter conditions. This remarkable process concentrates the sugars, acids, and extracts in the berries, thereby intensifying the flavours and giving Icewine its immense complexity.

The entire vineyard is carefully covered with netting to protect the sweet ripe berries from ravaging birds. Nevertheless, some of the crop is inevitably lost to wind damage.

The grapes are often painstakingly picked by hand in their naturally frozen state, ideally at temperatures of –10 to –13°C (14°F to 9°F), which sometimes forces harvesting in the middle of the night. Yields are very low, often as little as 5–10 percent of a normal yield. The frozen grapes are pressed in the extreme cold, often in the middle of the field to ensure that they don't defrost. Much of the water in the juice remains frozen during the pressing, and only a few drops of sweet concentrated juice are salvaged from each grape. If the grapes are allowed to warm during pressing, the juice will be diluted, affecting the quality of the wine. It is also critical to monitor the Brix level of the juice being extracted to ensure the highest quality. The juice is then fermented very slowly for several months and stops naturally at approximately 10–12 percent alcohol.

The quality of Icewine is determined primarily by the temperature at harvest.

Icewine tastes intensely sweet and flavourful in the initial mouth sensation. The balance is achieved by its acidity, which creates a clean, dry finish. The nose is reminiscent of lychees, and the wine tastes of tropical fruits with overtones of peach nectar and mango.

Historically, Icewine was first made in Germany in the mid-1700s. The quality of Icewine is primarily determined by how low the temperature drops at the time of harvest, resulting in high extract, fullness, and concentration of aroma in the final product.

The water in the berry is frozen and forms ice crystals which separate from the sugars, acids, and flavour components. Once pressed, the ice crystals begin to melt, and therefore it is critical to monitor the Brix level of the juice being extracted to ensure the highest quality.

Icewines exhibit fresh, crisp, resonant flavours and aromas with a highly intense backbone of acidity, which cleanses the palate and gives the wine depth, longevity, and a long, almost "peacock" aftertaste.

Another major characteristic of Icewine is its naturally high acidity, a direct function of cool-climate viticulture regions. It is this acidity which distinguishes Icewine from most other dessert wines, and, when in ideal equilibrium with the

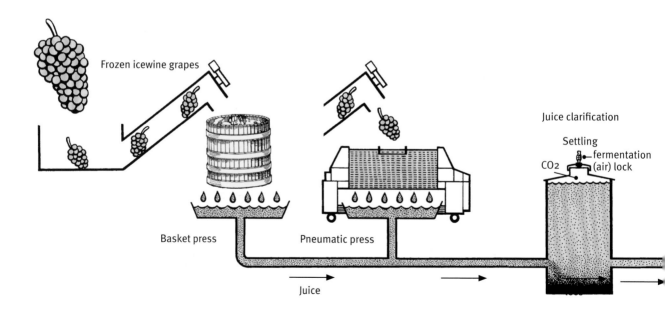

Frozen icewine grapes

Juice clarification

Settling

CO_2 — fermentation (air) lock

Basket press

Pneumatic press

Juice

intensity of sugar created by the natural freezing process, is what makes Icewine such a unique and truly great wine.

German law reclassified Icewine in 1983, establishing –7°C (19°F) as minimum harvest temperature, and a must weight of 125° Oechsle.

The other important aspect of making Icewine is the pressing off of only the sweetest juice while the grapes are still naturally frozen (first pressing) and the termination of pressing as the juice starts to become diluted. The dilution is created by heat generated by the friction from the pressing which melts the frozen grapes.

An interesting paradox of a great Icewine is that it can be consumed shortly after bottling or aged for well over 20 years. Youthful Icewines are fresh and clean on the finish, whereas older Icewines tend to be heavy and stronger in flavour, and linger on the palate longer.

Canada is blessed with cold winters. Yet weather is always a variable, as in 1997, when a mild winter brought on by El Niño almost ruined the prospects for Icewine in Canada.

Harvest
December to January

Harvest Temperatures
–10° C to –13° C (14°F to 9°F)

Picking
Hand or machine harvested (exclusively)

Naturally frozen on the vine

Normally throughout the night (coldest part of the day)

Yield
Extremely low (5 to 10 percent of a normal harvest)

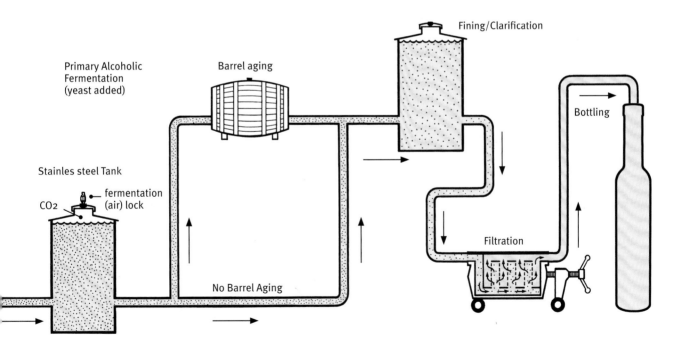

Ice and Water

Water and ice cover three-quarters of the earth's surface, mostly in the oceans and polar ice caps, but also as clouds, rain, snow, rivers, dew, etc. Continuously moving through the cycles of evaporation, precipitation, freezing, and run-off, water is integral to every living thing.

The freezing point of ice, used as a standard for measuring temperature, is 0°C (32°F). Ice expands in the act of freezing (hence bursting pipes), becoming less dense than water.

Ice exhibits itself in many ways, from tiny frost flowers on a sunlit window to towering icebergs. It is critical to the production of one of Canada's unique gifts from nature, Icewine.

When water reaches 4°C (39°F), it begins to expand. In other words, the density of water reaches a maximum at 4°C (39°F); below and above this temperature, the density of water decreases. This unusual property of water is what allows ice to float. Because water freezes below 4°C (39°F), i.e., at 0°C (32°F), ice is less dense than water. The reason for this apparent anomaly is that, at 4°C (39°F), water molecules are packed as tight as possible. When water is exposed to cold temperatures the random molecules suddenly jump to attention, forming millions of pristine hexagonal crystals in a crystal lattice structure, like ice and snow, which are both significantly less dense than liquid water. Any attempt to push them closer together, such as by lowering the temperature, only makes the water molecules push back harder, i.e., they repel each other.

So at 0°C (32°F), water can be ice or liquid water, and it will take significant amounts of energy transfer to change it from water to ice, or from ice to water. This is why a few cubes of ice can cool a whole glass of water.

Ice cubes freeze on the outside first (pull a tray out of the freezer after an hour or two, and you can push your finger through to the still-liquid centre). As water cools to freeze, the air dissolved in the water gets trapped as small bubbles between the crystals of ice. As the cube becomes solid on the outside, these small bubbles combine to make larger bubbles surrounded by walls of ice. The interior of the freezing compartment (inside the ice cube) is almost always well below water's freezing point of 0°C (32°F). This holds true even if you were to drop an ice cube into liquid nitrogen at –195.5°C (–320°F); the ice cube would cool to –195.5°C (–320°F).

Ice has many unusual properties; it has a volume per mole that is less than 10

percent larger than that of liquid water into which it melts, with the result that ice cubes float near the surface of water, with about 10 percent of their volume above the surface and 90 percent below. It is common knowledge that the portion of an iceberg that one sees floating in the ocean is only 10 percent of the iceberg.

Imagine a world where ice did not float. If ice sank, it is very likely that ice skating would never have been invented—a very unfortunate circumstance for Canada and its national sport, ice hockey, another Canadian icon. And if ice did not float, lakes would take forever to freeze from the bottom up making hockey a very different sport.

The ability to skate on ice is related to an effect known as surface melting—a net result of friction. Friction can generate enough heat to melt a thin layer of ice in contact with the skate. Surface melting occurs when the molecules on the surface become disordered and liquid, like at a temperature below the normal melting point of a solid. Contact with another surface (such as the metal of a skate) will influence this surface melting, since now the water molecules on the surface can bind to the metal surface atoms as well.

Another use of ice, originally employed by the Inuit and Eskimos to create igloos as homes, is the more recent creation of Ice Hotels. Canada has its own unique Ice Hotel in Quebec.

Ice Crystallization

To understand Icewine we must also understand freezing and the formation of crystals. A crystal is a material in which the molecules are lined up in a specific way (called the crystal lattice).

There are seven or more types of ice; the two we are concerned with are I ice and Ih ice. Ice can assume many different crystalline structures, more than any other known material. At ordinary pressure the stable phase of ice is called I. There are two closely related variants; ice Ih is ordinary ice, also referred to as hexagonal ice Ih (in the diagram below), which has hexagonal symmetry. Cubic ice has a crystal structure similar to diamonds.

As a crystalline solid, ice is considered a mineral. Minerals are chemically hydrogenous, with an organized structure of natural, inorganic origin. Ice fits this description, although generally no one thinks of water in this way.

Each oxygen atom (represented by red balls in the diagram below) inside the ice Ih lattice is surrounded by four other oxygen atoms in a tetrahedral arrangement. Each water molecule forms hydrogen bonds to its four nearest neighbours in a tetrahedral arrangement with one proton occupying each hydrogen bond. The tetrahedral bond geometry explains the openness and relatively low density of the ice Ih structure. The density of ice is dramatically less than that of water, due to the regular arrangement of water molecules via hydrogen bonds.

Water can take three forms: gas (vapour), liquid (water), and solid (ice). The graph (opposite) shows the phase diagram of water. The point at which ice, water, and water vapour can coexist is at a temperature of 0.01°C (32°F) and is referred to as the triple point of water. Water is the only substance that we commonly experience near its triple point in everyday life.

I presented a paper on this subject as my thesis to the Academie Internationale du Vin, in Geneva Switzerland, December 2005. Contained in the research material is information that sheds light on the process of ice crystallization and the subsequent production of Icewine.

However, I am not qualified to explain it sufficiently so I have provided abstracts from several studies below to shed light on the process of ice crystallization and the subsequent

ICE Ih CRYSTAL LATTICE

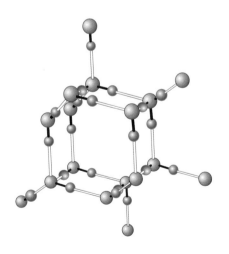

production of Icewine. You will quickly see how very complicated these various scientific processes are. Water and aqueous solutions have a strong tendency to cool below their melting point before ice begins to form; this is often referred to as supercooling. For example, although the melting point of ice is 0°C (32°F), water may be cooled significantly below 0°C before ice formation occurs. One effect of ice crystallization in an aqueous solution is to remove water from solution. The remaining liquid becomes more concentrated, and a two-phase system of ice and concentrated solution then coexists. As the temperature is reduced, more ice forms and the residual unfrozen liquid becomes increasingly concentrated. This is the basic principle in the production of naturally frozen grapes on the vine to produce Icewine.

During the freeze-thaw cycle[2], cells are subjected to a multiple of stresses including thermal, mechanical, chemical, and possibly electrical. Freezing tolerance in temperate plants such as grapevines is not simply a function of the minimum survivable temperature—the lowest for a grapevine is –18°C (0°F)—but involves a genetically programmed, integrated process which may alter the minimum survivable temperature.

The freezing of plant tissues and cell suspensions involves the redistribution of water with respect to both physical state and location. The location of ice formation may be either extracellular or intracellular and is strongly influenced by the cooling rate. It is at the cellular level that an understanding of the freezing process must begin.

PHASE DIAGRAM OF THE THREE STAGES OF WATER

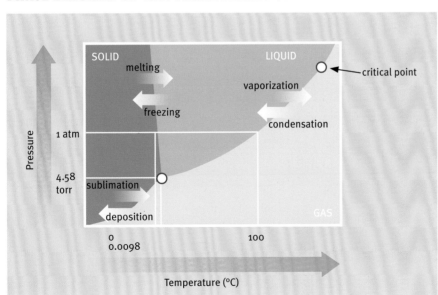

The basic structure and organization of most plant tissues and cells dictate to a large extent the site of initiation of ice crystallization, subsequently determining the course and location of cell-water freezing. Crystallization of the water inside the cell may occur by internal nucleation or by penetration into the cell by external ice crystals.

I believe it is this penetration of the ice crystals into the cell that provides much of Icewine's additional sensory aromas and profile. This freezing, termed "intracellular freezing," is considered to be lethal to the cell. Ice kills. Every cell in a grapevine is a squishy bag of water, with just a few other chemicals. If this water freezes, jagged crystals of ice appear, and slash and tear at the cell's fragile walls.

Within the cell, proteins unwind their complicated loops and become flaccid.

The presence of ice exclusively in the regions of the tissue outside the cell is termed "extracellular freezing." Extracellular ice formation imposes a dehydrative force on the unfrozen solution of the cell. During the extracellular freezing in plants, water will move out of the cell to the extracellular solution and form ice crystals.

Briefly, during cooling of a cellular suspension both the cells and the suspending medium initially supercool. Subsequently, ice formation occurs in the suspending medium at a temperature dependent on the freezing point of the juice in the grapes. Ice formation results in the exclusion of solutes, such as sugars and acid solutes, and hence a concentration of the partially frozen solution. Ice formation and the resultant solute concentration will continue until the water in the unfrozen portion is in equilibrium with that of the ice.

Ice formation in the extracellular solutions and the subsequent dehydration of the cell results in the concentration of both intra- and extracellular solutes.

Hermann Müller-Thurgau (1850–1927) (the grape varietal was named after him) made significant advances in describing intracellular ice formation and demonstrated that ice formed within cells at rapid cooling rates, but extracellularly at slow cooling rates. Müller-Thurgau noticed that tissues need to be supercooled before ice formation would occur inside the tissue, and that there was no injury when held at these sub-freezing temperatures in the absence of ice. He showed that the rate of thawing was of little or no consequence to the survival of most plant cells and that the temperatures at which lethal injury occurred correlated with the conversion of the majority of tissue water into ice. He argued that cell injury was primarily due to dehydration.

The formation of ice crystals seems to be as much due to the lack of heat as anything else. So why would ice crystals expand, requiring greater space than the

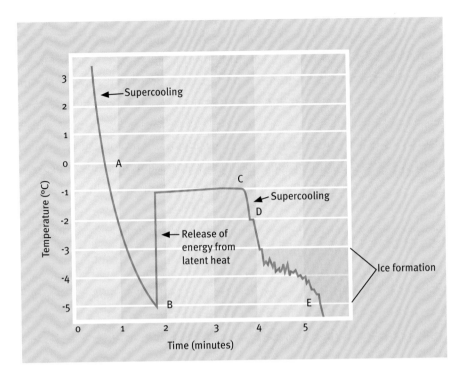

Temperature of cells in fruit during freezing. (B–C) Release of heat during freezing in cell walls and intercellular spaces. (C–D) Supercooling. (D–E) Small heat spikes released during intracellular freezing. (After Brown et al. 1974.)

liquid state? Look at a drop of water and look at the same water molecules represented as snow. Snow, as any skier will tell you, takes up much more space. When you melt several feet of snow you end up with only a few inches of water.

During the initial phase of heat loss from tissue, when the temperature drops below the freezing point without ice forming (A), the liquid is said to be supercooling. As the temperature drops further, ice forms in the intercellular spaces, and heat energy is released as a result of the latent heat of fusion of water. Heat of fusion is the energy which is withdrawn to solidify a liquid or added to melt a solid. The heat of fusion of water is 79.72 calories/gram.

At this stage, the temperature of the liquid inside the cell (or juice within a grape) reflects the balance between heat gain from ice formation and heat loss to the environment. As a result, when ice first forms, the temperature rises rapidly (B), and remains at that level until all the extracellular water is frozen (C). When that occurs, heat release stops, and the temperature begins to fall again. The release of heat energy during ice formation (B to C) is the basis for the common practice of irrigating crops with water during frost: as long as the water continues to freeze extracellularly, it releases heat that prevents intracellular freezing (see "Frost Protection" below).

The formation of ice within the intercellular spaces of cells that are sensitive to freezing is not lethal, but extended exposure to freezing temperatures causes water to move through the plasma membrane from the unfrozen protoplast to the cell wall, causing ice crystals to grow within the intercellular spaces. This slow dehydration concentrates solutes within the protoplast, depressing the freezing point by 2 to 3°C. As the temperature continues to drop, a second phase of heat-release water is detectable (D to E). This phase reflects a series of small freezing events: each "spike" of heat release is thought to represent the freezing of cell protoplasts and coincides with loss of viability. The formation of ice crystals on cell walls or in the protoplasm requires the presence of ice-nucleation points on which crystals can be initiated and grow. Ice cannot form by itself; it requires something to "germinate" from. In the case of a snowflake, that "germination" occurs around a dust particle or bacteria.

Plants produce compounds that protect cells against intracellular ice formation. Some of these compounds, such as sugars, amino acids, and other solutes, induce supercooling in the plant's tissues. Overwintering plants like perennials in cold climates also produce antifreeze proteins. These compounds provide freeze tolerance by inhibiting ice crystal growth and the nucleation of ice crystals.

Antifreeze proteins don't function like antifreeze used in cars. Antifreeze proteins work at the molecular level, coating ice crystals and literally blocking their growth.

Because of how they interfere with ice growth, antifreeze proteins can control recrystallization, a phenomenon familiar to anyone who has tasted crunchy flakes of ice in ice cream. A carton of ice cream may have originally been frozen quickly at a low temperature, the ideal condition for the water in the cream to turn to ice in minute crystals. However, if the temperature rises outside the freezer, water molecules can migrate and clump into larger crystals. If they get large enough, they change the texture of the ice cream from creamy to icy, something we have all experienced and not been happy about.

The process of making Icewine requires actual freezing to occur at temperatures of –8°C (18°F) or lower. This should not be confused with spring frost or the first frost, which is cold temperature occurring either in the spring or late fall. Early spring frost causes serious damage to plants, which is explained in detail in "Frost Protection."

In late fall these same frosts actually contribute to the crystallization of starches in apples which generally give apples from cool-climate regions more flavour. However, I repeat, this has nothing to do with the making of Icewine, which requires actual freezing of the grapes generally in the months of December and January with mid-winter temperatures of –8 to –13°C (18°F to 9°F).

Cold Hardiness

In the quest (research) to better understand the process of ice formation in the physical production of Icewine, I also discovered some very interesting information on cold hardiness.

The single most important factor for any plant to survive winter is its ability to prevent ice forming inside its cells. The instant an ice crystal forms inside a plant's cell, that cell is killed. It is a matter of preventing ice formation inside the cells. To accomplish this, water in the cells of hardy vines is permitted to slowly leave, freezing just outside the cells as crystals of ice. As the water leaves a cell, the dissolved sugars left behind becomes more and more concentrated. The lower the temperature, the more water will exit. This means that during times of extreme cold the consistency of the cell sap will change from being syrupy to being like solidified honey. In spring the cells in the grape vine rehydrate themselves by re-absorbing the water that froze just outside of them during winter. Simultaneously the grape vine itself simply tolerates the cold because the cell has hydrated.

It is the formation of ice, and not the low temperature, that kills the plant; however it is this formation of ice that is the principal agent in the making of Icewine.

Freezing tolerance in temperate plants such as grapevines is not simply a function of the minimum survivable temperature but involves a genetically programmed, integrated process[3].

A significant component of winter hardiness is the capacity to undergo cold acclimation. Grapevines, similar to many other temperate perennials, can alter their tissue and cellular freezing tolerance upon exposure to low freezing temperatures. Cold acclimation is the biological and physiological process associated with the increase in cold tolerance. Grapes rely on photoperiodic cues that signal the end of the active growth season and initiate the developmental and physiological changes necessary to promote cold acclimation and increase freezing tolerance.

Historically, cold acclimation and freezing tolerance were associated with the cessation of growth and the gradual transition from the heat of summer to the cold of winter. In cool-climate viticultural areas this transition becomes a critical factor in the production of the inherent acidity that is so fundamental to the production of Icewine.

Freeze-tolerant cells prevent ice from forming in the cell when water outside the cells freezes, causing water from inside the cells to move outside to form more ice. The water moving out of the cells through osmosis reduces the amount of water within the cell, concentrating sugars and other solutes inside the cell, forming natural antifreeze.

The hardiness of plants increases in the fall and early winter in response to shortening day length and/or low temperatures. The development of hardiness in the fall and early winter is a slow, gradual process. The loss of hardiness in late winter and early spring depends on temperature. In general, tissues or organs that are actively growing are least hardy. This situation occurred in Niagara in spring 2002 when actively growing vines were damaged by a sudden temperature drop in March after plant activity had commenced.

Freezing causes a complexity of changes in living cells, and some cells have an incredible ability to prevent or survive those changes. Where a plant is able to grow is determined in large part by its tolerance to environmental stresses like freezing.

During and after freezing, a plant cell's survival is threatened by cellular dehydration, mechanical disruption, hypoxia, and the direct thermodynamic effects of low temperature on metabolism. In freeze-resistant cells, scientists suspect that there must be a mechanism of protection, a complicated situation that is almost impossible to understand by physiological and biochemical analysis. However, it may be possible to use genetics to experiment with an affected gene to learn how the affected gene prevents winter injury.

The reason some insects and plants freeze in the winter and come back to life in the spring, versus what happens to human beings, is tissue damage[4].

Water outside of cells that turns to ice in certain insects and plants appear to freeze solid in winter. If the water inside their cells froze, the cells would explode like a bottle of water left in the freezer and the organism would die.

Freeze-tolerant plants and insects keep the water inside their cells from freezing, something human organs and tissues are not programmed to do. Because human cells live in a controlled 98.6°F and are destroyed by freezing, this is a real stumbling block in efforts to store donor organs for transplant operations. And another reason why humans find it difficult to tolerate picking Icewine grapes at −10°C!

Frost Protection

Although grapevines have their own genetically programmed systems to protect them from freezing damage, proper site selection, specific crop and soil management practices, and taking action when frost warnings are issued can improve frost protection.

There are two types of frost: advection frost and radiation frost.

Advection frost occurs when cold air blows into an area to replace warmer air that was present before the weather change. Advection frost is associated with moderate to strong winds, no temperature inversion, and low humidity. Often temperatures will drop below 0°C (32°F) and stay there all day. It is difficult to protect grapevines against advection frost.

Radiation frost is characterized by clear skies, calm winds, and temperature inversions. Radiation frosts result from heat losses in the form of radiant energy. Under clear nighttime skies, more heat is radiated away from a vineyard or field than it receives, so the temperature drops. The temperature falls faster near the radiation surface, causing a temperature inversion to form (meaning that temperature increases with height above the ground).

Eventually, if you measure high enough, the temperature will reach the point where it begins to decrease with height (a lapse condition). The level where the temperature profile changes from an inversion to a lapse condition is called the ceiling. A weak inversion (high ceiling) occurs (see graph, page 66) when the temperatures aloft are only slightly higher than near the surface. When there is a strong inversion (low ceiling), temperature increases rapidly with height.

ADVECTION FROST

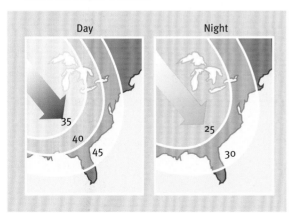

RADIATION FROST

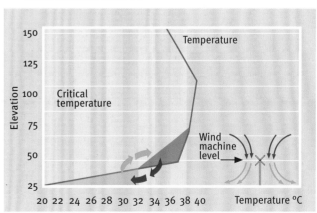

The most recent and current low-tech application is the use of wind machines during an inversion for prevention of winter injury during the winter months which might register –20°C at ground level and can cause damage to the grapevines. On cold winter nights growers use wind machines to circulate warmer air above to raise the temperature at the plant level and prevent freezing of the cells and winter injury. (See wind machine diagram, page 65.)

A totally different situation occurs in the spring wind—machines and irrigation can both be used. By irrigating plants when the temperature is expected to briefly drop below freezing, we can prevent spring frost damage. Irrigation works because of a thermodynamic property called the "latent heat of fusion." Water can exist in both the solid and liquid phases only at 0°C (32°F). So, if you chill liquid water, it will keep dropping in temperature until it hits 0°C (32°F). Then it will stay at 0°C (32°F) as it begins freezing and will not drop below that temperature until all the water has turned solid. After that, the temperature will keep dropping until it reaches the ambient temperature, which may be substantially below freezing.

So long as plants are irrigated with liquid water that subsequently freezes, the buds get no colder than about 0°C (32°F).

If the temperature is expected to dip below freezing for a short time, growers spray water on the exterior of the plant, allowing it to freeze, which will keep the buds at 0°C (32°F) and unfrozen in the centre. The freezing of the water gives off 79.72 cal/g of heat as the latent heat of fusion (see page 60). The time of protection

FORMATION OF INVERSION

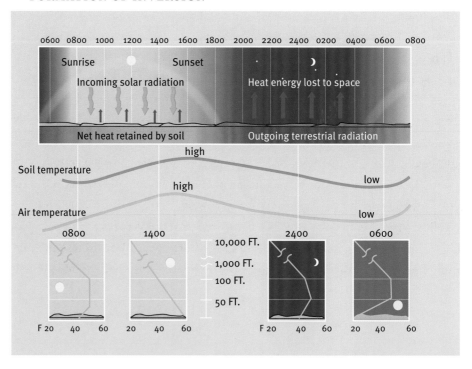

can be extended by spraying the fruit using a sprinkler, forcing the exterior of the buds to stay liquid and solid at the same time. However, if the temperature will stay below the freezing mark for an extended period, say several hours, then this strategy will not work; eventually, all the water will freeze. The plant will also freeze, then drop to the ambient temperature, ruining the buds and/or blossoms.

Wind machines in a vineyard for prevention of winter injury.

As explained earlier, low temperatures injure plants primarily by inducing ice formation between or within the plant cells. The area around the cells usually freezes first around 0°C (32°F) since it contains clean water. The water within the cell contains dissolved substances (minerals, salts, etc.) and, depending on the solutes and their concentration, can lower the freezing point of the cell several degrees. Frost-hardy plants have higher concentrations of solutes than frost-sensitive plant species. The freezing point within the cell may be further reduced when freezing occurs around the cell since water from within the cells exits and condenses on the growing ice crystals, which can be several thousand times larger than the cell. This continues up to a point without damaging the cell; however, below a certain point ice crystals will form within the cell. Ice formation within the cell damages the cell membrane, causing it to collapse and become incapable of moving water back into the cell. In frost-hardy crops, the cell membrane and its contents are more elastic and remain so even during freezing. This allows frost-hardy plants to resume functioning (metabolic activities) once the ice melts and water moves back into the cell.

Snowflakes

Although snow is not a functional part of Icewine production, I wrote this section on snowflakes because the winter vineyards are usually covered by deep snow and because I love to ski in deep powder. A good snow cover is very effective insulation for grapevine roots during extreme low temperatures.

These frozen crystals of all shapes and sizes float down and accumulate. The white fields resemble diamonds glittering in the sun…their existence and the fact that no two snowflakes are alike is a fascinating story [5].

For water to freeze, the water molecules need to slow down and touch something solid, called a nucleator. The nucleators most commonly found in clouds are dust particles and bacteria.

Scientists believe dust and bacteria blown off plants and thrown into the air by ocean waves produce rain and snow. The bacteria contain a molecule that attracts water. The nucleators are very, very small. The job of the nucleator is to start the snow crystal. The process of building a crystal starts when water is attracted to these tiny nucleators. Other water vapour molecules in their supercooled state will find this crystal and attach to it. The process of building a crystal is slow. After one ice crystal forms, it splinters into fragments, which serve as seeds for more ice crystals. The snowflake's six-sided shape comes from the hexagonal lattice structure of an ice molecule. This is a three-dimensional hexagon (see page 56).

Ice crystals are extremely sensitive to a variety of conditions, including temperature, air currents, and humidity. A crystal needs atmospheric conditions of −15C° (5°F) to grow. The colder the temperature, the sharper the ice crystal tips. I believe that this same phenomenon of sharp tips in ice crystals puncturing cells and cell walls of grapes yields extraordinary flavours in Canadian Icewines.

At warmer temperatures, the ice crystals grow slower and smoother, resulting in less intricate shapes. Differences in the macroclimate on each side of the ice crystal produce the asymmetrical shapes.

How a crystal grows is determined mostly by the amount of water available and the temperature with an influence by the atmospheric pressure and the electrical charge. Once the crystal starts it is still subjected to the same forces that the water vapour molecules are subjected to. The crystal can continue to be blown about for minutes to hours before falling to the ground. At different temperatures, fresh water molecules will attach to the crystal at different locations and "grow" differently[6].

There are texts that delve into the growth and types of crystals. However, because I love skiing and spend a lot of time in the snow, we will focus on only those types of crystals which form snow. The snowflakes are now on the ground piling on top of each other. The weight of the upper snowflakes will press down on those underneath, packing the snow. With all of the crystal shapes, initially the snow pack contains a lot of air. Over time the snow pack will compress making it denser. The density of freshly fallen snow can vary widely depending on the type of snow crystals that have fallen and the air temperature at ground level. Machine or manmade snow is done with the clouds taken out of the equation. But what is needed to make snow is pretty much the same. There is still the need for water, cold temperatures, a nucleator, and time to

form the crystal. But like fake Icewine it is just not the same. Anyone who has skied deep powder will attest to that, just as anyone will attest to the highly refined quality of Icewine naturally frozen on the vine.

Snow being white is really more of a question about the properties of light than it is the properties of snow. Light coming from the sun appears white to the human eye. This white light is really a composition of many different colours of light (red, yellow, etc.). If this white light is passed through a prism the colours will break apart and can then be seen by the human eye. It will look like a little rainbow. Snow crystals have a lot of flat reflective surfaces (the faces or facets). So since white light hits the snow, white light is reflected. Hence, snow appears white. As a snow pack reaches higher densities the absorbsion of red light is greater. A blue tinge will be more visible because not enough red is being reflected to maintain the light as white. You will see blue because the colour composition of light is now made up of more blue than red and blue stands out the most. However, the density will be high enough that technically it's no longer a snow pack. It would be a glacier or ice pack.

EDUCATION

*Every great viticulture and winemaking region
in the world is associated with institutions of
higher learning…as is now the case with Canada.*
—Dr. Donald Ziraldo

Top left: Niagara Culinary
Institute; top right: The Cool
Climate Oenology and
Viticulture Institute.

The Cool Climate Oenology and Viticulture Institute (CCOVI) is on the Brock University campus in Niagara, Canada. The CCOVI building was named Inniskillin Hall. This state-of-the-art teaching and research facility officially opened on June 11, 1999.

CCOVI's mission is to meet the research and education needs of the cool-climate wine growing and producing regions of the world. Its roles are to pursue the groundbreaking research and leading technologies necessary to maintain and enhance the competitive position of Canada's grape growers, vintners, and related professionals, and to foster partnerships. CCOVI has incorporated biotechnology labs, taking the best features from clonal selection, plant breeding, genetics, and other disciplines. Genetic engineering, as a positive tool in the natural control of diseases, offers many possibilities.

Niagara Culinary Institute at Niagara College is a natural complement to CCOVI since it provides a wine education component through its culinary program. Culinary tourism by international visitors is a critical factor in the recognition of our Icewine.

The recent renaissance of the Vinland Research Station will add additional capacity to the research and innovation capacity of the Niagara Region.

SCIENCE

Scientific Icewine Concepts and Facts

BY DR. KARL J. KAISER, BSC, LLD

In 1981 or 1982, I joked with Ewald Reif, one of our German grape growers at that time, about making Icewine. In 1983, Andreas Gestaltner, the Austrian winemaker working at Hillebrand Estates Winery, dropped by Inniskillin and asked if I would make Icewine.

That same year, I was talking with another Austrian countryman and winemaker, Walter Strehn of Pelee Island Winery. Out of curiosity, and for the novelty of it, we both decided to try the Icewine experiment and left grapes hanging on the vine that year—Pelee's with nets and Inniskillin's three rows of Vidal without. The outcome is easily guessed, and also documented in John Schreiner's book, *Icewine: The Complete Story.*

Well, we learned from that experience. By 1989, when Inniskillin was represented at the prestigious Vinexpo in Bordeaux for only the second time, Donald Ziraldo was prepared with a few bottles of our 1987 Vidal Icewine. Donald had a fortuitous meeting with Jacques Puisais, one of the founders of l'Academie Internationale du Vin and an enormously respected wine authority from France.

When he tasted our '87 Icewine, M. Puisais announced that he considered it one of the five best dessert wines in the world. Luckily, he had a huge number of followers at the show who doted on his every word. This encouraged us to officially enter our 1989 Icewine during the 1991 Vinexpo. And the rest, as they say, is history.

Today, Icewine has taken the Canadian and Ontario wine industry around the globe and become a serious business. In the early '90s Tony Aspler, Canadian wine writer and author, told me to "run with it." I did. He has since graciously written in the *Toronto Star* that "Canadian Icewine has become a global icon and it's because

of your efforts, Karl. By winning Le Grand Prix d'Honneur at Vinexpo 1991 for your Inniskillin Vidal Icewine 1989, you single-handedly brought the world's attention to Canadian wine and introduced wine lovers everywhere to Canada's gift of winter."

The success of Canadian Icewine has also triggered much scientific research into the Icewine process and production. I have worked closely with Dr. Debbie Inglis of Brock University's Cool Climate Oenology and Viticulture Institute, located in Ontario's Niagara Peninsula, on several such research projects, to gain a scientific understanding of the changes that occur in the juice before fermentation and during its transformation into the "nectar of the gods."

This chapter is meant to explain some of the "mysteries" and concepts behind Icewine making, and provide a better understanding of Icewine from a winemaker's perspective. I would like to thank Dr. Inglis for her co-operation and help, Tony Aspler for his encouragement and kind remarks, and John Schreiner for providing a comprehensive historical overview of Icewine production and explaining how it differs around the world.

Throughout the 1600s and 1700s, Europe and North America experienced extremely cold weather, wiping out vineyards in the Loire Valley and Austria during the "Little Ice Age" or "Maunder Minimum."

At the very end of this cold era, a new wine style—Eiswein, or Icewine as we call it in Canada—was developed, most likely by accident. German historical records assign Eiswein production to various dates and places. But the most commonly accepted is 1794 in Franconia, Germany.

It is likely that vintners were caught by an early freeze, or cold snap, when the grapes were still on the vines. The winemakers made the best of a bad situation by pressing the frozen grapes, and the first Icewine was created. However, since early Icewine production happened only by chance if extreme weather occurred, Icewine was not produced regularly throughout the nineteenth and twentieth centuries.

Since there were no specifications for harvest temperatures, many of the wines produced prior to 1971, and some before 1982 (when parts of the 1971 German Wine Law was revisited), were not true Icewines in the current sense and definition.

Those years between 1971 and 1982 were detrimental to the prestige of Icewine in Germany since it had been associated with the terms of Spätlese and Auslese—sweet wines that are really late-harvest wines—although the wine law of 1971 had already given Eiswein its own Präedikat, or category. However, there were references to Spätlese Eiswein, Auslese Eiswein, and also Beerenauslese Eiswein, but not Eiswein in the pure sense. It was not until 1982 that Eiswein was granted its own quality category equal to that of Beerenauslese in the German "Wine Law." In Austria, on the other hand, Julius Hafner from Mönchhof claims that his family made the first "intentionally, deliberately" made Icewine in Austria in 1971 and all other Icewines prior to that were "freak Icewines." (John Schreiner)

Nevertheless, since 1982/83, Eiswein's star started to rise again. I had the opportunity to taste a few very old German Eisweins and they were magnificent and quite obviously true Eisweins, with, however, rather low alcohol levels.

John Schreiner reports that Dr. Hans Ambrosi (co-author with Dr. Helmut Becker of Der Deutsche Wein) is called the father of German Eiswein by some of his peers. In 1991, during the Cool Climate Symposium at the University of Mainz, Germany, I was introduced to Dr. Ambrosi by the only American Master of Wine at that time, Tim Hanni of Napa Valley's Behringer vineyards. Dr. Ambrosi gave a seminar about Eiswein at the symposium and claimed he had been making it in the state cellars at Eltville since 1966. He and I enjoyed extensive conversations about Eiswein, and he was intrigued about our Canadian Icewines.

Today, after 23 tries and 22 successes in Ontario since 1983, I list my top observations about Icewine:

- Netting the grapes allows harvesting into the winter.
- The sugar level of the grapes in autumn has no influence on the sugar level in the Icewine juice. It's the unique process that determines the Icewine juice. It's the temperature at harvest and pressing that determines the sugar level in the juice.
- The high acid is critical to balance the high sugars of Icewine.
- An "off taste," also called a "frost tone," is a matter of personal taste.
- Early bottling, when the wine is very "reductive (fresh)," helps to preserve the necessary youthful freshness and reductive character of the Icewine. Icewine stored for a long time before bottling tastes tired and dull.
- Icewine is ready for consumption immediately after bottling and changes only very slowly during aging.

Liqueur Wines and Mistelles

Liqueur wines and Mistelles are alcohol-rich and mostly sweet wines, very common in the Mediterranean area. They usually have 15 percent actual alcohol, but not more than 22 percent, often ranging between 17 and 20 percent. Fermentation is either completely inhibited, or stopped, by the addition of alcohol (grape brandy), leaving much sugar unfermented.

Typical examples are port, Madeira, Marsala, Pineau des Charantes, and Samos. Frequently, Muscat varieties are used in Italy and Southern France.

Natural Sweet Wines

Natural sweet wines distinguish themselves from other sweet wines in that all the alcohol and unfermented residual sugar in the wine originates from the grape juice. Frequently, these wines are made from late-harvested grapes, dehydrated grapes, or Noble Rot (*Botrytis cinerea*)–infected grapes.

A typical late-harvest wine, whether sweet Spätlese or Auslese, qualifies as natural sweet wine if the wine's fermentation was stopped by chilling it. On the other hand, a wine fermented dry and then sweetened with a "sweet reserve" up to 15 percent of the volume (i.e., unfermented juice is added) would have a different composition and, although produced from fresh grown grapes, would not be called a natural sweet wine. (This type of sweetening a finished wine with unfermented grape juice is commonly used in Germany.)

Natural sweet wines include a wide category of wines, including table wine or quality wine, as long as the sugar in the final wine originated in the original juice. Natural sweet wines typically have more fructose than glucose in the remaining unfermented sugar. The fermentation process can explain this ratio: since almost all wine yeast is glucophilic, which means it ferments glucose faster than fructose, the leftover sugar is mostly fructose. Since fructose has a very high relative sweetness of 17 compared to 10 for sucrose and only 7 for glucose, a wine with a higher proportion of residual fructose will be noticeably sweeter than one with an equal proportion of glucose and fructose making up the residual sugar, even if the overall sugar levels are comparable.

We can also differentiate "Great Natural Sweet Wines" from "Natural Sweet Wines" with three distinct groups: air-dried/Passiti, Botrytis-affected wines, and Icewine. PASSITI: Produced abundantly in warm climates, wines made using air-dried grapes are made from grapes that are dried on the vines, laid on mats or straw, or hung on racks in greenhouses to dry. These Passiti or Straw wines, quite common in Mediterranean areas, are very old. For example, Reciotto wine (Masi) from the Verona area dates to Roman times. Its nearly dry version, Amarone, is a more recent development.

Passiti wines are delicious and can live many years, but often lack acidity. In the Middle Ages and earlier, high-alcohol wines were the only wines that could be kept without turning to vinegar. Methods such as late harvesting, or adding raisins, were often employed to achieve high sugar and hence high alcohol, which would preserve the wine.

BOTRYTIS-AFFECTED WINES: These wines are made from grapes in which a fungus, called "Noble Rot" in English, *Pourriture Noble* in French, and *Edelfaule* in German, dehydrates the grapes. In some grape areas with high humidity and fog patches in the fall, this fungus penetrates the skins and infects the ripe, sugar-rich grapes during warm and humid days (above 20°C [68°F] and more than 100 percent relative humidity). In addition to dehydrating the grapes, the mould also adds metabolites to the juice, hence changing the chemical makeup of the juice and its flavours. The Botrytis also adds its own flavours to the juice, and concentrates the acids.

The infected grapes are hand-picked and pressed, or, in the case of Tokay or Austrian Ausbruch, made into a paste and fermented with other wine.

The juice extracted for Trockenbeerenauslese is very, very sweet (the German minimum legal requirement is 150° Oe or 35° Brix, but usually the juice is much higher) and, depending on the extent of the Noble Rot infection, also exhibits high acidity. In this type of concentrated juice, the tartaric acid is usually in equal or greater ratio to the malic acid.

Jancis Robinson, in her 1998 book The Oxford Companion to Wine, describes the flavour of Botrytis wines as "honeyed[; they] can sometimes have an overture of boiled cabbage." Generally, Botrytis wines do not exhibit primary, varietal, fruit characteristics because the mould overpowers and replaces them, and the wines do not retain those fruit flavours for long. Because the mould subdues the varietal distinctions, many varieties of Botrytis wines taste quite similar.

Botrytis wines, like Ausbruch, Sauternes, Tokay, and Trockenbeerenauslese are very long-lived: I had a Chateau d'Yquem from the late nineteenth century that was superb. German Trockenbeerenauslese wines live as long and can easily surpass a human life span.

ICEWINE: The Oxford Companion to Wine (1998, p. 357) states that although Icewines "lack Noble Rot, or Edelfaule, character, which makes them easier to drink when young, and their high acidity makes them extremely refreshing, the majority of the Icewine producers in Austria do not want botrytis in their Icewines. Many do not produce Icewines in those years when there is botrytis on the berries and produce rather botrytis wines such as Beerenauslesen, Trockenbeerenauslesen or Ausbruch wines." The same is true for Germany.

Willi Opitz, a winemaker from Illmitz in Austria, sums it up as John Schreiner in his book *Icewine: The Complete Story* writes, "...a poor outlook for noble rot is a good one for Icewine, the reverse is equally true."

There are often reasons why Botrytis-infected grapes are not desirable for Icewine making. First, Botrytis-infected grapes do not hold well on the clusters, so there is a chance of losing most of them early. Second, even if they did hang until pressing, the yield would be extremely small since the berries are already dehydrated by the mould. Third, why wait for Icewine weather when one can produce outstanding Noble-Rot wines earlier? Fourth, why mix the incredible, clean, fruit-forward flavours of an Icewine with Botrytis flavours? Fifth, a fully Botrytised grape could not be made into a true Icewine since the juice is too sweet and cannot be frozen; hence it would not be an Icewine.

Icewine is made from the juice of grapes that have frozen naturally on the vine. The grape juice becomes naturally concentrated due to the freezing out of water from the juice. In general terms, freezing separates the water in the grape from the sugar, acids, and other flavour compounds. Unlike Botrytis wines, there is no contribution by *Botrytis cinerea*. Icewines are sweet, but exhibit a pure sensation of harmony between sugar, acidity, and fruit.

Since the grapes are pressed while still frozen, the water remains as ice and is discarded, while only intensely sweet and concentrated amounts of juice are retained. Because of Icewines' concentration of fruit flavours, they are often called "incomparable," true, noble, sweet wines that have no peers.

Icewine Vintages

In a good growing year when grapes have a lot of flavour in autumn with good acidity, Icewines will reflect this quality. While the quality of regular table wines depends on the sugar, acid, and ripening state at harvest time, the quality of Icewine does not depend on these factors as much because of the concentration effect in the grapes throughout the fall and winter. The only difference might be in very hot growing years, in which the acidity in the grapes would decrease and the grapes would tend to have a softened skin, resulting in a shortened hang-time on the vine.

In general, however, Icewine grapes experience a concentration of sugar, acids, and flavours regardless of their makeup during regular autumn harvest. Differences are more subtle from vintage to vintage. With our Canadian winters, we can say that we have only excellent Icewine vintages and difficult vintages.

Some difficult vintages are largely the result of very warm winters, rainy periods in January, and/or having to wait into February or even March before harvesting. These weather patterns are often associated in Canada with El Niño. During El Niño years, the tradewinds in the Pacific Ocean, which normally blow west, are reversed and blow east, piling very warm surface water on the southern North American, northern South American and middle American west coasts, which then warms the air. The Arctic jet stream is then divided, keeping cold Arctic air in the extreme northern regions of the Arctic. Eastern Canada then experiences mild winters.

The only truly difficult Icewine vintages are the ones where the temperature barely reaches −8°C (18ºF) or slightly lower, the temperature required by VQA regulations to harvest Icewine grapes. Since 1983, Niagara vintners have not missed a single Icewine vintage due to temperature. In most years, Ontario, and specifically Niagara, has ideal conditions. Only with El Niño weather patterns do we experience difficulties from lower

FROST-FREE DAYS IN THE NIAGARA PENINSULA (30-YEAR AVERAGE)

Location	Last Spring Frost	First Fall Frost	Frost-Free Days
Power Glen	May 8th	October 13th	157
Niagara Airport	May 1st	October 22nd	173
Vineland: Rittenhouse	April 30th	October 19th	171
Vineland: Station on Lake	April 28th	October 22nd	175

yields because of the grapes dehydrating, shrivelling, and dropping to the ground.

In Niagara, typical El Niño vintages occurred in 1988 (last picking was on February 4, 1989), and in 1997 (in which a devastating six-day January 1998 ice storm brought freezing rain to eastern Ontario and Quebec [the Niagara Peninsula had warmer weather] and the last harvest had to wait until February 5, 1998). The 2001 vintage had the longest wait, stretching out over several months until the last harvests took place on March 4–5, 2002.

Ideal Icewine harvests occur from the middle of December through the first half of January. Normally, a good skiing winter is a good Icewine winter.

La Niña, a weather pattern that alternates with El Niño, is characterized by strong westerly tradewinds that help bring the cold Humbold current water from the Antarctic to the surface, creating cold air above. The jet stream dips further south and brings this cold Arctic air to more southerly regions. La Niña winters in Ontario and eastern Canada are cold, but good for Icewine harvests.

ICEWINE HOURS OF −8.0°C DURING THE WINTER MONTHS OF THE 1999, 2000, AND 2001 VINTAGE IN THE NIAGARA PENINSULA, ON[1].

December 1999	22.6	December 2000	122.7	December 2001	2.5
January 2000	244.2	January 2001	44.3	January 2002	6.4
February 2000	48.3	February 2001	38.3	February 2002	31.7
Total 1999	315.0	Total 2000	205.2	Total 2001	40.6

Optimum Harvest Parameters

Ideal Icewine conditions include a dry and moderately cold December, with a few partial freezes and real freezes of the grapes, in which we can harvest some of the crop; then a snow cover over Christmas, followed by a cold stretch over two weeks with daytime temperatures between –9°C (16°F) and –11°C (12°F).

Mechanical harvesting of grapes illustrating vibration of the trellis to shake off grapes from vine.

Ideal parameters for the pressed juice are between 38° and 42° Brix, juice yield around 150 L per tonne (October estimate) for Vidal and 125 L per tonne for Riesling with an ideal titratable acidity of 10–12 g/l tartaric acid and pH between 3.1 and 3.3.

Yields in the vineyard should be no more than 7 tonnes/acre for Vidal and 5 tonnes/acre for Riesling as calculated in October.

INFLUENCE OF HARVEST DATE ON ICEWINE

Hand harvesting of grapes at night.

VERY EARLY (NOVEMBER): Most winemakers agree that a very early freeze (–8˚C [18ºF]) in November does not generate juice that produces the highest quality Icewine, although the yields are high. Since the grapes at this early date have not gone through the significant physical and chemical changes that occur as grapes hang on the vine and experience multiple freeze–thaw cycles, Icewines resulting from the earlier harvested grapes do not appear as complex as Icewines made from fruit harvested in December through January. Although November harvests in Ontario are rare (the first one was recorded in 2005), they are quite common in Austria and British Columbia.

VERY LATE (FEBRUARY/MARCH): The grapes in February/March are usually very dehydrated. The fruit has experienced a fair amount of rain, leading to grape breakdown and shrivelling, requiring colder temperatures to freeze out the water. Many grapes have fallen to the ground by this time or have been eaten by wildlife (birds, deer, coyotes, raccoons, etc.). Juice yields usually are quite low at this late harvest date.

IDEAL: The optimal harvest time for Icewine grapes is mid-December to mid-January, with at least one freeze–thaw cycle prior to harvest to allow for the development of more complex flavours, while still retaining sound, disease-free fruit that is hanging well.

MINIMIZING BIRD PREDATION

In general, from early December until Christmas, the birds in Ontario that will feed on Icewine grapes are mainly starlings. They are less voracious when there is no snow since they can access plants and seeds. However, an early snow forces the starlings to look for alternative food sources, and grapes become very attractive. In late winter, with very little food available for the starlings, flocks can clean out a vineyard in no time.

To protect the grapes, auditory bird-scaring devices are used in conjunction with propane canons in the fall. Because these devices do not have the same effect in winter, nets are our best bet.

If the snow reaches the nets that cover the grapevines, birds will sit on top of the snow and pick the grapes through the netting. Therefore, nets must be long enough to be tied under the grape vine canopy and prevent the birds from gaining access to the grapes from below. Netting mesh size is also an important factor in protecting the grapes. Since a significant portion of the grapes are machine harvested in Ontario now, it is important to have a mesh size large enough to let the berries fall through, but small enough to keep the birds out. A perfect mesh size is about 2.5 cm square.

Other types of nets, often used in Europe and other parts of North America, are often shorter and applied only as curtains. These are not effective in Ontario.

Icewine-producing Countries and Acreages

Among "Old World" wine-producing countries, most northern and continental countries can and do produce Icewine. Proximity to the ocean discourages Icewine production because of moderating, maritime climates; however, continental climates are beneficial for Icewine production because of the cold winters.

In Europe, Icewines are made in Germany, Austria, Slovenia, Switzerland, Hungary, Slovakia, and others. These products are the result of recent winemaking trends, with the exception of Germany where Icewine has the longest tradition.

CANADA, ONTARIO: Ontario wine-growing regions are located in a continental climatic area that is greatly influenced by the moderating effects of great masses of water. Lake Ontario provides this moderation for the Niagara Peninsula growing area, and Lake Erie provides this effect for Pelee Island and the Lake Erie North Shore growing areas. All grape-growing areas are situated at a latitude north of 43°N.

CANADA, BRITISH COLUMBIA: The Okanagan Valley in British Columbia is about 150 km long and stretches in a north–south direction, from Winfield, north of Kelowna, to the United States border. The Okanagan is a semi-desert climate, which needs irrigation for all fruit. It is well-sheltered from the east and west by substantial mountains, which cause a rain shadow from the west. Its latitude is north of 49°N.

UNITED STATES, WEST: The interior of Washington State, which is the main grape-growing area of the state, has a semi-desert climate similar to the Okanagan Valley. It lies in the rain shadow of the Cascade Mountains, and it too needs regular irrigation. Winters can be cold and arrive as early as December.

UNITED STATES, EAST: Ohio, Pennsylvania, and New York State, where most of the Eastern American Icewine is produced, have a climate similar to Ontario's. Some areas are favoured with the moderating effects of the Great Lakes, while other inland areas are not.

GERMANY AND AUSTRIA: Icewine and Beerenauslese have the same Brix requirements (29.58° Brix).

Ideally, grapes for Icewine should:

- be an aromatic variety
- have high acidity and low pH
- be late ripening

WINE GRAPE ACREAGE 2004

Canadian Icewines vs. German, Austrian, Swiss Icewines —
potential acreages:

	Acres	Ha
Ontario	10,500	4,900
B.C.	5,500	2,900
Total Canada	16,000	7,800
Germany–16.5x	272,000	128,000
Austria–7x	115,000	50,000
Switzerland–2x	31,500	14,800

🦋 have strong physiological properties such as strong skins and stems

🦋 be relatively disease-resistant.

In Ontario, Vidal is the predominant variety, followed by Riesling, Cabernet Franc, and Gewürztraminer. In B.C., Riesling, Ehrenfelser, Chardonnay, Chenin Blanc, and others make up most Icewines. Of Canada's Icewine production, Ontario contributes about 75 percent, with 75 percent of that made from Vidal.

Vidal, or Vidal Blanc, is an interspecific cross from the 1920s between Ugni Blanc (Trebbiano in Italy) and Rayon d'Or (Seibel 4986). It is very winter hardy and quite disease-resistant, with good acidity and fruity, aromatic flavours.

Vidal's full scientific name is Vidal 256, named after its breeder, Jean L. Vidal, who was director of the Fougerat Station at Bois-Charentes (Charente, France). In Canada, every VQA wine must be varietally labelled.

Many German Icewines are blends, with Riesling being only a small portion of that blend. Dr. Ambrosi reports that many German vintners have denounced Riesling as being too acidic and unsuitable for Icewine. Nevertheless, Dr. Ambrosi believes that Riesling is perfect in a ripe year with no extreme acidities.

In Austria, Welschriesling and Scheurebe (Saemling 88) are quite commonly used. Besides Gewürztraminer, Sauvignon Blanc, Chardonnay, and even Pinot Blanc and some red varieties are used for Icewine.

In Germany and Austria, an Icewine does not need to be varietally labelled and can be any blend (without declaration of the varieties).

Cryoextraction

The word "cryoextraction" comes from the Greek word "kryos," meaning frost or cold. Cryoextraction implies that the application of cold or freezing will freeze out or separate and extract some substances, hence concentrating the remaining liquid portion. Icewine is made from grapes naturally frozen on the vine; the freeze–thaw cycle can be considered natural cryoextraction.

Freezing grapes artificially is called artificial cryoextraction and is not permitted in Canadian or European Icewine production.

The principal behind cryoextraction is physical-chemical, and involves "freezing-point depression" due to a solute. The freezing-point depression of a liquid refers, in this case, to a solute. A solute is a substance that is dissolved in a liquid, specifically water. Table salt, sea salt, and sugar are solutes. At sea level, pure water freezes at 0.0°C (32°F); however, sea water does not freeze at this temperature because its dissolved salt lowers (depresses) its freezing point. We make use of this phenomena in the winter when we thaw ice on our driveway or sidewalk by sprinkling salt on it.

Freezing of the Grape

The juice in a grape comprises water (70 to 80 percent), sugars (18 to 24 percent), and fruit acids (0.8 to 1.2 percent). The sugar and acids are solutes that lower the freezing point of the juice in the grape, so it does not freeze until the temperature reaches –7°C (19°F) or –8°C (18°F). Grapes that are less ripe and have the lowest Brix (sugar), for example, 17.0° Brix, will start to freeze first at –6.0°C to –7°C (21°F to 19°F). This gradual differential freezing is used sometimes in the Sauternes region and exploited as partial artificial cryoextraction when the grapes are chilled to a temperature where only the unripe ones freeze.

Very ripe berries need lower temperatures to freeze, which has implications for Icewine producers in Austria, for example, where the minimum sugar requirements for grapes are much higher than in most parts of Germany. Growers will need a much colder temperature to freeze their grapes than in the Mosel region, for example, where the grapes do not require as much sugar by law.

German wine law acknowledges this phemonenon of lower-sugar-content grapes needing less cold to freeze by allowing certain regions to produce Icewine from much lower Brix grapes and Icewine juice, since those grapes will freeze at a higher temperature.

As the water freezes out, the remaining juice becomes more concentrated and freezing slows; even colder temperatures are needed to continue freezing the grapes, which experience a continuous concentration effect.

Since more and more water becomes fixed as ice crystals in the grapes, the liquid becomes higher in sugar concentration and the extracted-juice yields decrease when pressing at lower and lower temperatures. The molecules responsible for the incredible aromas and flavours of Icewine aren't trapped in the water crystals; rather, they migrate into the highly concentrated juice.

When there is winter injury in any plant, ice crystals are formed in the plant cells, and these ice crystals will rupture the cell membranes and tissues, killing the cells. In Icewine making, we exploit this in the grapes. When they are pressed frozen, the embedded ice crystals rupture the grape, bursting the cells, and piercing the grape and skin, thus helping facilitate the release of the juice and flavour components. The process also releases more colour from the grapes' skins, making the Icewine juice darker.

This "helping hand" of ice crystals becomes obvious when making Icewine from red varieties such as Cabernet Franc. The juice of a grape of most red varieties is clear and colourless since the colouring matter, the anthocyanins, is embedded only in the skins. When making red wine, we ferment the skins with the juice at a relatively higher temperature (25.0 to 33.0°C) to extract the colour. This cannot occur in Icewine making since the grapes are frozen. Therefore, we count on the ice crystals to help release colour from the skins.

Eventually, when the temperature is below –14.0°C, no more juice can be extracted. The fruit acids are also concentrated, but a great portion of tartaric acid is lost since it precipitates as cream of tartar (K Tart.) in the grape, which is discarded. Malic acid, on the other hand, cannot precipitate as a potassium salt and seems to be fully recovered and in a titrated amount of, for example, 10.0 g/l of total acid (TA).

For example, if the grape juice had 20.0° Brix before freezing and had 10 g/l of acid, we would expect a 40.0° Brix Icewine juice and 20.0 g/l of titrable acidity. However, this doesn't happen because some of the tartaric acid is lost in the grapes, so a typical acidity in Icewine juice would be between 9.0 and 13.0 g/l in a 37.0° to 42.0° Brix juice, of which a great portion consists of malic acid. In very high Brix juices, the tartaric/malic acid ratios favour malic acid and lower tartaric acid, which makes Icewine more crisp and refreshing.

This might even suggest that Icewines made from extremely high-Brix juices are not as balanced.

On the other hand, grapes that have been fully Botrytised and already show over 40.0° Brix can not be made into a true Icewine because these grapes will not freeze (too much sugar); also the yield would be too low, and the process uneconomical.

Icewine Regulations

Technically, there are several differences in the legal requirements for producing Icewine in Canada versus Germany or Austria (see table, facing page).

In Canada and EU regulations, grapes can be partially or completely frozen in the vineyard several times prior to the actual Icewine harvest. The winemaker or processor makes a decision when to harvest as long as temperatures reach –8.0°C (18°F) in Canada (–7°C [19°F] in the EU) or colder during harvest.

We harvest and press less-concentrated juices for our other late-harvested wines, which include in Ontario and British Columbia: Late Harvest (LH) 22.0° to 26.0° Brix; Select Late Harvest (SLH) 26.0°to 30.0° Brix; Special Select Late Harvest (SSLH) 30.0° to 34.9°Brix; Icewine 35.0° Brix and above.

Minimum Brix		
Germany:	29.58 Brix	= 125 Oechsle
Mosel:	26.40 Brix	= 110 Oechsle
Austria:	29.58 Brix	= 27.0 Klosterneuburger
Canada:	35.0 Brix	= 148 Oechsle

Minimum Cold		
Germany:		−7°C (19°F) or colder
Austria:		−7°C (19°F) or colder
OIV Resolution 2003:		−7°C (19°F) or colder
Canada:		−8.0°C (18°F) or colder

Germany and Austria: other sweet wines can also be produced from partially frozen grapes or prolonged pressing. Although in the EU wines can generally be made only from fresh grapes, there are exemptions for "wines of unique ripeness and type of harvest," of which Icewine is one example. (Frozen grapes are not considered fresh grapes, according to the EU standards.)

ACIDIFICATION

By law, Icewines or any other quality wine cannot be acidified with tartaric acid in the regions A and B within the EU. Citric acid can be added to a total of 1.0 g citric acid in the finished wine; this is not considered an acidification but a stabilization. In Germany and Austria, this legal handicap often leads to low-acid, not so well balanced Icewines, particularly Icewine made from high-pH, low-acid varieties.

Ontario and British Columbia have a great advantage, since we can add several acids, in addition to citric acid, to a total of 4.0 g/l of combined acidification (as the Canada–EU Wine and Spirits Agreement allows). For Riesling, this is usually not necessary, but for Vidal, Gewürztraminer, and Cabernet Franc, small acid additions are more often necessary. By adding acids, we achieve an improved balance in the resulting Icewines.

In 2003, a very hot year in Europe, up to a 1.5 g/l addition of tartaric acid was permitted for this one year only in some of the more northerly EU viticultural regions for all "quality wines."

Icewine Grape Harvest and Pressing

MACHINE HARVEST VERSUS HAND HARVEST

Machine harvesting is limited to flatter terrain and topographical profiles, but has the advantage that large acreages can be harvested quickly. Even short hours of harvest windows can be exploited for a quick gathering of the grapes.

In general, only the grapes fall through the nets, with the stems (stalks) remaining on the vines. Because the harvester shakes the vines and the whole trellis, about 10 percent of the grapes are lost before the machine can catch them. Marginally frozen grapes do not fall through the mesh very well and often get caught. However, at –10° to –11°C (14°F to 12°F) the grapes are like marbles, falling easily through the net and being caught perfectly for machine harvesting.

Machine-harvested Icewine grapes result in cleaner fruit with less debris since the blowers of the harvester remove fallen leaves and broken stems. Machine-harvested frozen grapes give a cleaner juice with lower levels of insoluble particles.

Nevertheless, hand harvesting is the traditional way of gathering grapes for Icewine. Although much more labour-intensive, the harvest has a much more emotional connection to the product. The nets must be slit underneath so the frozen grape bunches can fall through the openings to be collected in picking boxes. Since not all the grapes fall into the boxes, leftovers end up feeding winter wildlife.

PRESSING

In the making of Icewine, the frozen berries go directly into the press. Almost any press that delivers enough pressure can be used to press frozen grapes, but there are differences in the quality of the juice from different presses. Generally, presses that have a lot of moving parts (cages, chains, etc.), such as horizontal presses, give a "dirtier" juice with more sediment than presses with no moving parts, such as a basket press. High-pressure presses are preferred for speedy extraction and very "clean" juice.

When the juice is collected, often after hours of pressing, particularly with low-pressure presses, the lower the temperature, the slower the juice releases, the higher the Brix, and the lower the yield. The temperature of the juice at the press is anywhere from –8°C to –14°C (18°F to 7°F).

The horizontal pneumatic press utilizes an inflatable bladder running the length of the press along a central shaft. When the press is loaded, the bladder is in a collapsed state, tightly covering the shaft. The bladder can then be inflated inside the cage to press the grapes against the inside perforated wall of the cage.

Interestingly, more and more Icewine is being pressed in traditional basket presses. Basket presses can be utilized in the field as well, and are more flexible.

CROSS-SECTION OF HORIZONTAL PNEUMATIC PRESS

BASKET PRESS

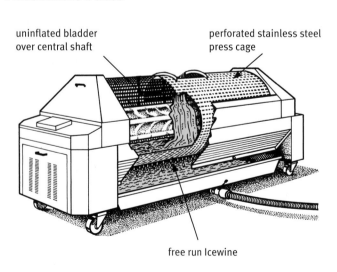

uninflated bladder over central shaft

perforated stainless steel press cage

free run Icewine

frozen Icewine grapes

Freshly pressed icewine juice.

CALCULATIONS OF ICEWINE MUST CONCENTRATION AS A FUNCTION OF PRESSING TEMPERATURE

The juice concentration from the pressed Icewine grapes is independent from the original sugar present in the grapes (must density) but strictly dependent on the pressing temperature.

The formula used to determine the concentration of Icewine must at various pressing temperatures is as follows (Wuerdig, Schlotterer, and Mueller, 1975):

Density 20°C/20°C (specific gravity)
= [21 + (17 × ΔT) × 10 − 3] + 1

Where ΔT (Delta T)
= 0.0°C − (pressing temperature °C)
And Oechsle degree (Oe°) = 21 + (17 × ΔT)

Example 1: press temperature at −9°C
ΔT   = 0.0°C − (−9.0°C) = 9.0
Density 20°C/20°C
    = [21 + (17 × ΔT) × 10 − 3] + 1
    = [21 + (17 × 9.0) × 10 − 3] + 1
    = [174 × 0.001] + 1
    = 1.174
Density = specific gravity
= 1.174 = 174 Oe° = 39.0°Brix

Example 2: press temperature at −7.0°C
ΔT   = 0.0°C − (−7.0°C) = 7.0
Oe°   = 21 + (17 × 7)
    = 21 + 119
    = 140 Oe°
    = 32.7 Brix

Example 3: press temperature −8.5°C
ΔT   = 0.0°C − (−8.5°C) = 8.5
Oe°   = 21 + (17 × 8.5)
    = 21 + 144.5
    = 165.5 Oe°
    = 37.84 Brix

Example 4: press temperature −10.5°C
DT   = 0.0°C − (−10.5°C) = 10.5
Oe°   = 21 + (17 × 10.5)
    = 21 + 178.5
    = 199.5 Oe°
    = 44.44 Brix

The juice will then be separated according to its Brix fraction. This provides the base to produce Icewines of more than one quality level (Brix). As stated in VQA regulations, the minimum combined tank average must be at least 35° Brix in Ontario and B.C. In Austria and Germany, the temperature must be −7°C (19°F) and the juice must have a minimum of 29.58° Brix (125 Oechsle in Germany or 27.0 Klosteneuburger degrees in Austria). In the Mosel, only 110 Oechsle (26.4° Brix) is required.

Above: the relationship between juice soluble solids measured as Brix or density vs. the pressing temperature of the Icewine grapes.

Winemaking (Oenological) Icewine Practices

THE JUICE

Juice collected from the presses has the temperature of the grape at the time of pressing. Since the pressing is limited from −8°C (18°F) (if higher, the grapes are not frozen) to −14°C (7°F), and since there is no juice extraction below −14°C, the juices can have temperatures only between −8°C (18°F) and −14°C (7°F) and Brix degrees between 35.0° Brix and 55.5° Brix. The yields are highest at −8°C (18°F) (less water is frozen) and lowest at −14°C (7°F) (almost all water is frozen).

JUICE TREATMENT

Since the juice, when collected, is cold, settling and clarification is very slow. In order to facilitate a more rapid settling, the juices are allowed to warm slightly as they are stored in the tanks. Other methods of clarification include centrifuging the juice or using rotary vacuum drum-filters (RVD). Sometimes the juices are racked a few times and, at the discretion of the winemaker, fined with bentonite and/or protein-based fining agents to remove particles and undesirable solutes in the juice prior to fermentation. Sulfiting the juice is also at the discretion of the winemaker. The opinion of each winemaker differs on juice treatments and each one has his or her own preferences.

ICEWINE JUICE COMPOSITION

After having analyzed virtually hundreds of Icewine juice samples from Riesling, Vidal, and Cabernet Franc (see table, page 183), we can generally say that Riesling has the most bracing acidity with a low pH. Vidal Icewine juice in general has similar acidity to Riesling but with higher pH. Gewürztraminer and Cabernet Franc have low acidity accompanied by a relatively high pH. The Icewine juices have enough nitrogen, and the majority of the acid is malic acid.

The analytical data shows that, in the Icewine juice, virtually all of the malic acid is recovered during pressing and almost all of the ammonia and amino nitrogen is recovered from the juice; the high amounts reflect the concentration effect in Icewine juice.

Much of the tartaric acid is lost in the grapes as cream of tartar (K+ Bitartrate) because of the freezing, which shifts the acid ratio strongly towards malic acid dominance. In a finished Icewine in which there has been no acidification with tartaric acid, the majority of the acid is always malic acid. Riesling Icewine, with its refreshing, bracing acidity, is an example of this. In most table wines tartaric acid is normally dominant.

When there is a significant acid addition necessary, done with tartaric acid (for example, Gewürztraminer and Cabernet Franc normally need a slight acid boost), the acid composition ratios are quite different, shifting the ratio to a more dominant tartaric acid.

This makes me wonder if some malic acid addition on Gewürztraminer or Cabernet Franc, rather than just tartaric acid additions, would make these Icewines more racy since they lack both acids.

The data in the table (page 183) shows that cream of tartar precipitation is dependent on (1) the pressing temperature, which implies that higher-Brix juices obtained at the colder temperatures have a higher malic acid ratio in the juice, since more cream of tartar precipitated in the grape, leaving little remaining tartaric acid; and

(2) pH. The pH has an enormous effect since the solubility of K+ Bitartrate is at a minimum at the midpoint between the pKa1 and the pKa2 of tartaric acid, which is at a pH of 3.65; it follows that grapes with high pH will lose more tartaric acid during the freezing process (chemical composition of Vidal Icewine juice and nitrogen usage during fermentation)[2].

Icewine Fermentation

INOCULATION

Prior to fermentation, the winemaker might create different blends with the various Brix-rated juices. Most Icewines would fall into the 37° to 42° Brix range. When the juices are to the liking of the winemaker, he or she brings the clarified juice to a temperature at which the yeast can ferment, between 13.0° (55°F) and 25.0°C.

The juice is difficult to ferment because of the high osmotic pressure on the yeast[3], so the winemaker uses plenty of yeast while applying the proper rehydration procedure, which is recommended by the manufacturer[4].

The winemaker can choose from many different yeast strains and follows the manufacturer's guidelines for the best results.

FERMENTATION

The fermentation of Icewines and other dessert or sweet wines is an extraordinary challenge for the wine yeast; sugar concentrations around 400 g/l represent an extreme stress situation for these cells. Because of the osmotic pressure placed on the yeast cells from all the solutes concentrated in Icewine juice, the yeast loses water by osmosis, shrinks in size, and some cells start to die.

The yeast must respond to this stress by producing glycerol to protect itself against further water loss, and this glycerol production is biochemically coupled to the formation of acetic acid [5].

This means that Icewines naturally contain higher levels of volatile acidity that adds to the increased titratable acidity we find. The combined effect of the increase in acetic acid and succinic acid, which amounts often to an increase in titratable acidity (T.A.) by roughly 2.0 g/l, is frequently responsible for making the Icewines more balanced and often helps to bring the Icewine into the minimum legally required total acid range in EU producing countries. (Recently, a visitor from Austria said this happened to one of his Icewines, which otherwise would have failed the legal requirements for the regulated minimum acidity.)

Using a particular Swiss yeast strain (W15 and W27), Swiss researchers showed that at a higher fermentation temperature of 30°C, the glycerol production is higher, along with an increased production of acetic acid (which increases the volatile acidity, or V.A.). As a compromise, for good glycerol production (increased mouth feel) and low acetic acid production, a fermentation temperature of 15°C (59°F) is appropriate [6].

Alcoholic Strengths—Today and Historically

In Canada, Icewines must have at least 7 percent actual alcohol and in the EU at least 4.5 percent alcohol. Today these alcohol levels can be achieved easily with modern, commercial wine yeast strains, but historically these alcohol levels were often not achieved, for two major reasons:

First, Icewine grapes have very few or no viable Saccharomyces wine yeast cells left on the grapes[7]. This is especially true for grapes harvested in January or later, as found in the study "Population Changes of Yeast Flora Associated with Vidal and Riesling Icewine Grapes—Across Four Successive Harvest Dates[8]." These researchers found that the Saccharomyces population diminishes as the winter continues. Grapes for Icewine were harvested at four different dates: 1st harvest: Nov. 12, 2002; 2nd harvest: Dec. 11, 2002; 3rd harvest: Jan. 7, 2003; and 4th harvest: Feb. 5, 2003. Again, differences were found between Vidal and Riesling. Overall, the natural flora became diminished as the winter continued but the most dramatic loss of natural flora was observed by the second harvest (Dec. 11, 2002).

Since Saccharomyces is the main yeast species responsible for wine production, historically, Icewine fermentations would have been sluggish or would not take place since the indigenous Saccharomyces population in the juice would have been so low or non-existent. Acid-forming yeasts or other opportunistic micro-organisms could then take over the fermentation and leave the wines with very low alcohol levels and off-flavours. This is not so significant with other sweet wines, such as those made with Botrytis grapes, which are also dehydrated but harvested early in the season (October or November). Today in the EU, wines that contain less than 4.5 percent alcohol are not legal any more and must be disposed of (as I was told has happened to a top Austrian producer recently with a Trockenbeerenauslese).

Recently, researchers in Canada[9] found that during the 2002 vintage, effectively no viable fermenting Saccharomyces yeast was present during spontaneous Icewine fermentation.

Although the natural yeast flora from Vidal and Riesling Icewine juices were different, spontaneous fermentations were delayed and slow, and provided a sensory profile that was different from that found in the inoculated fermentations. The natural flora produced a higher glycerol content in Riesling than when fermented with added yeast strains, whereas Vidal's glycerol contents were comparable.

The second reason for the low alcohol levels achieved historically in Icewines is that grape juices with high sugar exhibit high osmotic pressure on the yeast cells and cause a high mortality rate of the yeasts. Even if there were only a few viable cells of Saccharomyces yeast in Icewine juice, sooner or later the juice would probably be void of any of these viable cells because of the high mortality due to the high osmotic pressure.

Historically, we must assume that most Icewines had very low alcohol percentages and would often express off-flavoured aromas. I would postulate that prior to the use of modern active yeast strains, the Icewine juices had to be "luckily contaminated" and actually inoculated with yeast cells from the equipment and/or from lees residues from wooden barrels, as opposed to the Icewines being fermented with the indigenous yeast cells originally present in the Icewine juice.

Despite the fact that Old World vineyards might have had better indigenous flora than New World vineyards, we must conclude that the fermentations proceeded rather slowly and provided only very low alcohol with very mixed results. The odds were against a "sound and healthy" fermentation.

We must also assume that Icewine, as infrequently as it was made in the more distant past, if it was produced at all, would have been produced by only major and reputed domains and estates. These estates would have had good oenological knowledge and full-time winemakers who knew how to warm the barrels, cellars, and juice, and possibly also knew to select and nourish yeast cultures from their own in-house yeast strains. It was not until the latter part of the nineteenth century that Pasteur clearly elucidated the fact that yeast was responsible for alcoholic fermentations. Even in today's German wine law, as little as 4.5 percent alcohol level is required, indicating the historical difficulties associated with Icewine fermentation.

No doubt the onset and availability of the modern, active dry-yeast strains helped start the real "Icewine Bonanza."

Cold Stability

Although Icewines will have lost a great portion of the potassium ions and tartaric acid in the juice because of the cream of tartar precipitation in the berries, Icewine is still hard to cold stabilize. The very high specific gravity of the wine (leaving often 230–250 g/l of residual sugar) does make a tartrate stability very difficult in the final wine.

Facing page: Karl Kaiser examining Brix level of Icewine with refractometer.

Heat Stability

Icewines are not heat stable and normally need a fair amount of bentonite fining. In most cases, 150 g to 250 g/Hl is normal, but much higher amounts have been referred to.

Chemical Composition of Icewines

During the freezing process, both the sugar and the acids (tartaric and malic predominantly) are concentrated in the juice, the malic acid being almost fully recovered, but a fair amount of tartaric acid being lost in the grapes as cream of tartar, which shifts the acid dominance to malic acid.

The minimum Brix required by law (vqa standards) is 35° Brix for the juice in the fermenting vat. This minimum standard of 35° Brix was adopted for Canadian Icewine to match the requirements for an Austrian or a German Trockenbeerenauslese. We wanted to set our Icewine standard higher than the EU standard (at par with their top sweet wines). Inniskillin's Icewines are all in the 38° to 42° Brix range, with the majority between 39° and 41° Brix.

The resulting wines are around 10.0 to 10.5 percent alcohol and have between 190 and 220 g/l of residual sugar and a typical acidity between 10 and 13.0 g/l of titrable acidity. The increase in volatile acidity (acetic acid) does not lower the aromatic qualities of an Icewine but actually enhances the fruitiness. The overall increase of acidity by the yeast by about 2.0 g/l is a welcome factor and so is the extra amount of glycerol produced, which gives the wines increased body and mouth feel. A typical, excellent Icewine has about 10 to 12 g/l of glycerol and a "sugar-free extract" of about 30.0 g/l.

The high acidity pairs wonderfully with the high residual sugar to an extraordinary balance with a refreshing sensation[10].

Icewine Flavours and Aromas

There are many, many distinct flavours and aromas in different Icewines. Primary Icewine flavours and aromas are concentrated fruit characteristics. Wine writers have indulged in countless descriptions of these wonderful wines, and their interpretations are unique and interesting. However, all Icewines exhibit undistorted clarity in their aromas and flavours.

Icewine Styles

Ontario has two distinct styles of Icewines, especially in the Vidals. The "fat" style includes Icewines that show deeper colour, yet are often one-dimensional in flavour profile. This characteristic seems to be caused by a higher phenolic content, often associated with higher alcohol content.

The "slim" style includes Icewines that are more refined, and lighter in colour and alcohol, which achieves 10.0 percent or slightly above. These Icewines seem to have more finesse, since individual flavours come to the foreground. They are also more complex, with finer fruitiness and a variety of flavour profiles that also harmonize on the palate. The "slim" style is Inniskillin's forte.

Longevity of Icewines

How long do Icewines live? It's unclear how their longevity compares with the longevity of the best "Botrytis wines," which can easily age gracefully for 100 or more years. We do know that Noble Rot wines in Germany, called "Trokenbeerenauslese," have been made more frequently than Icewines in the history of wine, meaning that there are fewer records of Icewine's longevity. Much depends on the initial sugar concentration of the juice and the total acidity. It's a good bet that Icewines made from grapes with low pH, high acid, and reasonable alcohol could live for 50 years or longer if cellared properly and kept very cool (10° to 13°C [to 55°F]).

SPARKLING ICEWINE

The year 1998 was a great grape-growing year and an outstanding vintage, especially for red wines. The grapes were ripe and the acids were good. Forecasts for Icewine exports to Asia were very positive.

At Inniskillin, we netted an optimistic number of vines for Icewine. Although December was actually +3.7°C above normal, two days before Christmas and the last two days of December were ideal Icewine harvest days (between −9° [16°F] and −12°C [10°F]), as were the first sixteen days of January 1999. Excellent yields of extraordinary quality were harvested.

I thought about making Sparkling Icewine with some of this extra juice, but first had to work through the VQA to find an acceptable way to produce such a thing, keeping in mind that the carbonation (CO_2) had to come from the fermentation and not from a CO_2 injection; and that it was impossible to make Sparkling Icewine through a bottle fermentation knowing that a 9 percent alcohol base-wine Icewine would hardly ever be restarted for a secondary fermentation in the bottle.

So I came up with the alternative, making Sparkling Icewine in a Charmat tank.

This had to be done in one step, from the juice stage to the finished sparkling wine, instead of the usual two stages (juice to wine to sparkling wine) for other sparkling wines.

I had read that some Italian Spumante Prosecco wines were made that way to preserve extreme freshness, so I decided to try the same technology and use the same initial yeast culture. My research implied that a standard Charmat tank could be used, however, with an open lid until the alcohol reached approximately 9.0 to 9.5 percent. At that point the lid would have to be closed to trap the CO_2 from the last 1.5 percent alcohol increase. In other words, the original yeast would need to be viable enough to ferment to 10.5 or 11.0 percent alcohol.

The sparkling wine would have to spend some time on the lees to qualify for "Quality Sparkling Wine" status as laid out in the EU wine regulations. I convinced my colleagues in the VQA Board of Directors of the legitimacy of this process, and the rules we laid down are now in VQA legislation.

At Inniskillin, we have made this type of Sparkling Icewine every vintage year from 1998 until 2003, with the exception of 1999.

TASTE

The Taste
Experience

Riedel

On October 18, 1999, Riedel and Inniskillin conducted an Icewine atelier/workshop to create the ultimate Icewine glass. From the prototype (page 111, upper left) developed by Donald Ziraldo, Georg Riedel, and Karl Kaiser, an exquisite vessel emerged to deliver the ultimate experience of Icewine. The Riedel/Inniskillin Vinum Extreme Icewine Glass (page 111, centre) was created in 2001.

THE GLASS/PALATE

The wineglass performs a very important function; it is the vehicle by which we experience a wine's complexity and personality through our sense of smell and taste. The wineglass plays a vital role in shaping our experience and therefore our opinions and memories of a particular Icewine. Quality wineglasses offer quality experiences and enjoyable memories. Inferior wineglasses serve only to get an alcoholic beverage to our lips.

Quality in a wineglass is determined by shape. One glass brings out the wine's vibrant fruity aromas, while another thwarts them. A quality wineglass makes a wine's acidity taste refreshing and pleasing to the palate. An inferior wineglass makes this same acidity seem tart and offensive.

You can experience these not so subtle nuances for yourself by experimenting. Pour a wine from the same bottle into a variety of differently shaped glasses. Smell and taste each glass. You'll be amazed by how the same wine can smell and taste so different.

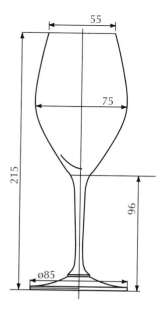

Left: prototype, Icewine glass; right, finished Vinum Extreme Icewine glass.

The shape of a glass influences the bouquet and perceived taste of wine. The grape variety is the key factor in determining the relationship between fruit, acidity, and alcohol. Additionally, the use of barrels has an influence on the tannin structure.

The quality and intensity of aromas are determined not only by the personality of a wine but also by its affinity to the glass shape. Bouquet can develop properly in a limited temperature range. Aroma refers to odorants derived primarily from the grape variety, while bouquet refers to scents that develop primarily during fermentation and aging. So a wine's aroma and bouquet are quite different. The level of alcohol in wine also affects the intensity of aroma and/or bouquet. The greater the alcoholic content, the heavier the aromas in the wine.

Temperature plays an important role in wine. Important as the shape of a glass is, it cannot function properly unless the wine is served at the correct temperature and in the right serving quantities. A cold temperature mutes aromas and flavours; a warmer temperature often enhances them. Icewine served at a very cold temperature, for example, will possess "closed" or subtle rather than robust aromas. Its taste will seem less sweet and more astringent. When this same Icewine is served at a slightly warmer temperature, its aromas can be full, bold, and rich: its palate full and luscious. Low temperatures temper the aromatic intensity, whereas high temperatures promote mainly alcoholic fumes and heavier aromas (high molecular weight) such as vanillin.

The effects of temperature on the sweetness of sucrose have the most practical significance at relatively low concentrations of sucrose. According to Riedel, the sweetness of sucrose increases by 40 percent as the temperature increases from 4°C

From left to right, Donald Ziraldo, Georg Riedel, Karl Kaiser.

(about refrigerator temperature) to 36°C (about body temperature). On the other hand, the sweetness of a lower sucrose concentration like the sucrose equivalent of 2 teaspoons of sugar in a cup of coffee increases by 92 percent (i.e., the sweetness nearly doubles) as the temperature increases from 4° to 36°C.

Sugars are the primary natural stimulus for the sweet taste in nature. Love of sugar is virtually universal among mammals. It has also been demonstrated that sweetness is liked before birth. The sugar molecule that is most important biologically is glucose. This molecule serves as an important energy source in the body and is the only energy source that can be utilized by the brain. This may explain our great love for Icewine.

The size and the shape of the glass can be fine-tuned to the typical aromas of a grape variety. When wine is poured into a well-shaped glass it immediately starts to evaporate and its aromas quickly fill the glass in layers according to their density and specific gravity. The lightest, most fragile aromas are those reminiscent of flow-ers and fruit. These rise up to the rim of the glass. The middle fills with green vege-tal scents and earthy, mineral components. The heaviest aromas, typically of wood and alcohol, remain at the bottom of the glass. Swirling the wine in the glass moist-ens a larger surface area, increasing the evaporation and intensity of the aromas. However, swirling does not blend different elements of the bouquet.

Each individual is the sovereign of his palate. The term palate is misleading for consumers and unfortunately widely used in the wine industry. The palate barely contributes to taste perceptions. Most of the gustatory receptors for sweet, acid, salty, and bitter are located on the tongue and upper larynx. However the term is widely used.

Wines smell and taste differently in a variety of glasses for several reasons. Physical movements and adjustments of head and body are controlled subconsciously. The shape of the glass forces the head to position itself in such a way that you can drink without spilling. Wide, open glass shapes require sipping by lowering the head, whereas a narrow rim forces the head backward so that the liquid flows because of gravity. This delivers and positions the beverage to different "taste zones" of the palate.

The resulting nerve impulse is transmitted to the brain at a speed of 400 m/sec, where it leaves a lasting first impression. In most cases we are disappointed if sweet fruit flavours are absent and tart components dominate the taste picture. The perception of taste (acid, sweet) is perceived on the tongue while the nose perceives the aromatic perceptions. We perceive aromas in the mouth through the retro-nasal route.

This is precisely where a glass can make a dramatic difference in conveying a wine's message. Every wine has its own unique blend of qualities: fruit, acidity, minerals, and tannin result from the grape variety and the climate and soil on which it is grown. The wine's aftertaste or "finish" plays an important role in the overall impression. The finish also strongly influences the design of the bowl of the wineglass.

To fully appreciate different grape varieties and the subtle characteristics of individual wines, it is essential to have a glass whose shape is fine-tuned for the purpose. The shape is responsible for the quality and intensity of the bouquet and the flow of the wine. The initial contact point depends on the shape and volume of the glass, the diameter and finish of the rim, and the thickness of the crystal. As you put your wine glass to your lips, the wine flow is directed onto the appropriate taste zones and consequently leads to different taste pictures. Once your tongue is in contact with the wine you also notice temperature and texture, often referred to as mouth feel and taste.

One of the most widespread "facts" about taste concerns the distribution of sensitivity to the four basic tastes: sweet, bitter, sour, and salty. Sweet sensitivity is at its maximum on the tongue tip and its minimum on the base of the tongue. Bitter sensitivity is

Taste zones of the tongue.

at its maximum on the base of the tongue and its minimum on the tip. Sourness sensitivity is at its maximum at the centres of the tongue edges and at the minimum on the tip. Saltiness is perceived approximately equally on all loci.

This so-called "tongue map" has been challenged by scientists; however, it is very much part of popular culture, particularly the perception of bitterness on the back of the tongue[1].

When food or wine enters the mouth, it contacts gustatory receptors (tastebuds) on the tongue and palate, producing sensations of sweet, salty, sour, or bitter. At the same time, volatiles rise through the oral and nasal cavities to reach the olfactory receptors located just under the eyes. The many distinct olfactory sensations produced are responsible for much of the sensory experience of eating. That is, when we eat, we both taste and smell foods. The combination of taste and olfaction is called flavour and we perceive it as being located in the mouth.

We believe that this localization is produced by the sense of touch. Taste sensations are not localized to the location of taste buds but, rather, to areas touched in the mouth. Thus during drinking and eating, taste sensations seem to originate from the entire inner surface of the mouth even though the taste buds are found only in certain places. This occurs because the brain uses the sense of touch to localize taste sensations.

Although we generally speak of tasting foods and beverages, much of the sensory input involved is actually olfactory. The good news is that taste is very robust across age. The bad news is that olfactory sensations do diminish with age.

HEALTH

Wine has always played an integral part in the health and happiness of mankind.

On Sunday, November 5, 1998, CBS's *60 Minutes* gave a phenomenal boost to the wine industry. The program revealed scientific evidence that moderate wine consumption with meals helps prevent heart disease. Morley Safer interviewed two scientists who found that despite similar fat intake, France's heart attack rate was one-third that of the United States. A key attributing factor is the French custom of drinking wine with meals. Antioxidants, in addition to alcohol, are likely to be responsible for wine's beneficial effects.

Commonly referred to as the "French Paradox," the phenolic compound resveratrol is considered one of the agents in wine that reduces cardiovascular disease and possibly certain cancers.

Phenols and polyphenols are complex substances found primarily in grape skins that give wine their characteristic aroma, flavours, and mouth feel. Because red wines tend to have longer skin contact during fermentation, they are higher than whites in phenolic compounds, including resveratrol.

Resveratrol is a natural fungicide in the skin of grapes. It provides protection for the grape in cool, damp climates. The more cool and humid the climate, the more resveratrol is produced to combat mildew, an interesting phenomena of cool-climate viticulture. Pinot Noir has high levels of resveratrol wherever it is grown. Wines from Niagara, Burgundy, Oregon, and New York have the highest levels, according to Dr. David Goldberg, Professor of Biochemistry, University of Toronto.

Resveratrol was used in ancient Japanese and Chinese folk remedies and was believed to reduce "bad" cholesterol and prevent blood clotting.

Icewine Martini

There will probably be a lengthy debate about the origin of the Icewine martini. It was first brought to our attention by a young Vancouver bartender who used it to win a mixology competition.

Our initial concern was diluting the purity of our Icewine; however, with the appearance of the Icewine martini in several trendy lounges, including L.A.'s Skybar and South Beach's Reds, we seized the opportunity to create our own Icewine martini.

CLASSIC ICEWINE MARTINI

Created at Opus Restaurant, Toronto.

2¾ oz. Iceberg Vodka (Canadian)
1¼ oz. Icewine
stirred not shaken
garnished with frozen grapes

The amount of Icewine can be reduced to increase the dryness of the martini.

FROSTBITE MARTINI

Created by Aaron Merlino, bartender at the
Four Seasons Hotel in San Francisco.

INGREDIENTS
2 ounces Vodka
½ ounce Inniskillin Icewine
½ ounce white cranberry or white grape juice
1 teaspoon lemon juice
1 teaspoon simple syrup
Superfine sugar
A twist of lemon
1 teaspoon Crème de Cassis
Five or six frozen grapes

Fill a shaker with ice. Add the vodka, Icewine, juices, and syrup. Give it a good shake and pour into a chilled martini glass rimmed with sugar. Twist the lemon over the drink to release its oils, then garnish the rim of the glass with it. Add the cassis and let it sink to the bottom of the glass. Serve the frozen grapes in a dish on the side.

Makes 1 drink.

Facing Page: hand-blown "Dragon" ice crystal by Canadian glass-blower Brad Copping.

Taste Anatomy

The tongue is covered with a variety of papillae that give it its bumpy appearance. Taste is produced by the dominant allele, T. (An allele is any of the alternate forms of a gene that may occur at a particular locus). Individuals with two recessive alleles, tt, are nontasters and individuals with two dominant alleles, TT, are tasters.

Tasters have more taste buds than nontasters. In addition, tasters with more taste buds perceive stronger tastes.

Supertasters have the largest number of taste buds, nontasters the smallest. For example, the average number of taste buds per square centimetre was 96, 184, and 425 for nontasters, medium tasters, and supertasters, respectively. The supertasters' fungiform papillae (mushroom-shaped projections on the tongue) were smaller and had rings of tissue around them that were not seen on the fungiform papillae of nontasters. Some people are natural "supertasters," while others lack the anatomical characteristics. These anatomical differences may prove to be a better indicator of genetic status than the taste differences[2]. However, this evidence is quite controversial since the term supertaster only refers to the ability of a taster to taste a bitter compound called PROP and maybe capsaicin (hot pepper). This ability is somewhat correlated with the perception of other bitterants but not with aromatic perceptions, 80 percent of which we perceive in the mouth.

ICEWINE FLAVOUR WHEEL

The Icewine flavour wheel developed by Shari Darling is a tool that provides us with the ability to articulate our experience of the aroma, taste, and flavours of Icewine by providing a wide range of words and terms from which to choose.

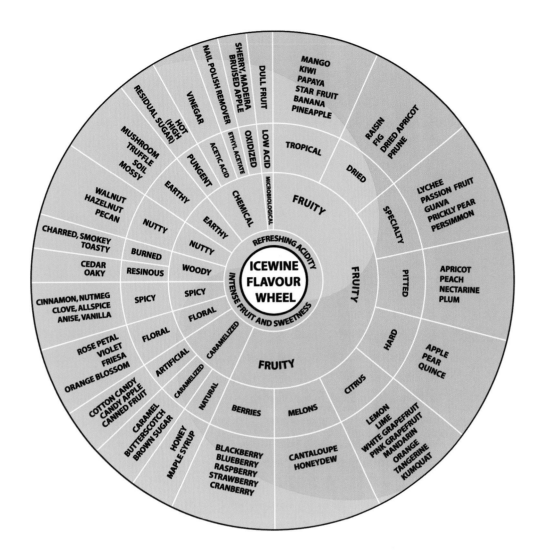

ICEWINE FLAVOUR WHEEL

WHY THE YIN-YANG COLOUR SYMBOL?

The flavour wheel itself speaks to Icewine in its entirety. The yin-yang symbol within the circle represents the two primary taste sensations found in quality Icewine: refreshing acidity (green) and intense sweetness (gold). The moving shape of the yin and yang gives us a sense of the continual movement of refreshing acidity and intense sweetness experienced when we sip Icewine. Yin harmonizing with yang; yang with yin.

Icewine
with Food

IZABELA KALABIS-SACCO,
INNISKILLIN RESIDENT CHEF
(1988–2006)

In loving memory,
June 25, 1963 – September 11, 2006.

This is the story of one woman's affair with Icewine and food. Izabela Kalabis-Sacco became a chef because she was inspired by food, primarily with a glass of wine, which is the way most people enjoy food around the dinner table. She grew up in the Niagara-on-the-Lake village of St. David's, graduated from the University of Guelph with a major in French, travelled to Paris to study at La Varenne, and apprenticed at small restaurants in France, where she developed a true passion for the culinary arts.

Donald Ziraldo caught wind of this amazing local culinary talent, and upon returning from Europe, Izabela began working at Inniskillin.

As new resident chef for Canada's leading winery, Izabela delivered countless themed lunches in the winery Loft. She was inspired by the local harvests and whenever possible sourced her produce from the surrounding gardens, orchards, and fields to create dishes to partner with the wines of the same region.

Classically trained, Izabela was a bold chef who never put parameters on what she could create and accomplish. She continued to impress with well-crafted and stylish lunches, dinners, and events at the winery; designed a successful Wine & Food Adventure Card Series; developed countless wine and food recipes for magazines and was featured on many TV shows as Inniskillin's resident chef.

During her tenure, Izabela developed her appreciation of Icewine as a culinary ingredient, enabling her to discern the complex flavours and interplay between food and Icewine.

Izabela valiantly fought breast cancer and, although she did everything in her power to halt the disease, she died at 43. Izabela leaves a lasting legacy with her creative Icewine and food pairings and a zest for enjoying food and wine that leaves us refreshed, delighted, and inspired anew. The following pages are a reflection of Izabela's work.

Icewine and Food

The Niagara region provides many products, from orchard fruits to field vegetables, garden herbs to country meats, farm-raised poultry to new-world cheeses, field berries to world-class wines. All of this produce is gathered to create a world-class culinary collaboration that depends as much on the production of its ingredients as it does on the transformation of those ingredients into a delicious dish. Growing, harvesting, preparing, presenting, and eating foods from the garden are all phases of the same activity. For both fine wine and good food, it's about the unbroken arc from the earth to the table.

It makes sense that Niagara's climate and unique geographical elements influence not only the locally grown fruits and vegetables but also the wine grapes. The slow ripening season produces lively acidity balanced with sweetness and deep, rich flavours. For example, peaches, the quintessential Niagara fruit, when fully ripened are bursting with intensely sweet peachy flavours balanced by a lively acidity so the flavours awaken your palate. Tomatoes grown in fields adjacent to the vineyards express a similar balance of acidity and sweetness.

The analogies between food and wine and a sense of place are endless. Food, like wine, needs to be grown in healthy soils with enough sunlight and rain; it also needs to be produced in small yields with careful harvesting methods. Just as there are different grape varieties, there are different varieties of tomatoes, peppers, peaches, and strawberries. The same elements of soil, climate, vegetation, and landscape that provide a region with its diversity in wine are all things that offer variety in our food.

Celebrating Icewine and local food reflect culinary culture, regionalism, and a healthy sense of pride in our agricultural heritage. This is why seasonal, perfectly ripe produce, whether peaches, grapes, apricots, or pears, is best accompanied by a local wine.

In fact, the fall season is a great time to experiment with Icewine because fall fruit and Icewine is a match made in heaven. It's also when our appetites crave something savoury; foods that naturally bring a fuller quality to our dining pleasure.

Like Chateau d'Yquem, the great Sauternes, Icewine has an extravagant sweetness and intensity. Its magical balance of acidity and sweetness give it a texture that is surprisingly elegant and sets it apart from other sweet dessert wines. This balance of perfectly ripe fruit flavours and aromas with acidity for depth and complexity makes Icewine the least cloying of all dessert wines and more likely to marry well with a wider variety of foods.

Unlike many other distinctive foods and wines, Icewine is not an acquired taste. One sip immediately reveals its extraordinary appeal. On the palate it begins with a mouthful of nectarine, apricot, and pineapple flavours layered with the added richness of lychee and honey. No other wine comes so close to the pure expression of dark honey without honey's sugary fierceness.

The question remains: How to best enjoy a glass of Icewine? Unfortunately, perhaps because of its price, its elite food partners, or the fact that it is so different from other table wines, Icewine often confuses traditional wine drinkers. Pity, because Icewine is one of the world's most diverse wines.

The potency of flavour in each sip and its hypnotic aromas means Icewine can be sipped with hushed reverence as you would a good port; a wine made for wine's sake. Icewine is the perfect dessert all on its own.

However, like many other complex and intense wines, Icewine can also be enjoyed with food. Icewine offers a powerhouse of flavours with a graceful style to marry deliciously well with many, many foods.

Icewine is a perfect dinner partner because it has the ability to change over the course of a meal. Like all wines, once poured into a glass Icewine comes alive. Some of Icewine's changes over the meal can also be due to nose fatigue: when certain aromas dominate, our ability to appreciate them at their peak fades while more subtle aromas begin to reveal themselves.

Vidal is the quintessential grape variety for making Icewine in Canada. It dominates with an intensity of apricot and pineapple and the zing of dark honey that plays throughout the long finish. It's the purity of fruit flavours that makes Vidal outshine all others and is reason for its duality. The flavours pair eloquently with fresh local dishes like Summer Berries with Chilled Icewine Cream, Peaches with Raspberry-Icewine Purée, and Apple-Grape Tart with Icewine Crust. Vidal's fig and tangerine notes end rich and creamy to enhance more exotic dishes like Foie Gras with Granny Smith Apples and Blackcurrant Reduction.

Vidal Icewine aged in oak takes on characteristics of almonds, vanilla, and warm bread. The result is a wine with greater depth and more opportunity for pairing with dishes like Bosc Pear Mousse with Chocolate Biscuit and Caramel Sauce. The oak not only brings out the biscuit flavour but also rounds out the earthy lingering caramel notes. An Oak-aged Icewine also embellishes the caramelized character of a grilled dish such as Icewine Marinated Pork Medallions with Corn-Crusted Onion Rings.

When bubbles and Icewine come together, as in Sparkling Icewine, the result

is sleek and elegant with beautifully defined tropical fruit, ginger, pear, and lemon-lime flavours that turn smooth and polished on the finish. Sparkling wine fans get the best of both worlds. The bubbles cut through the richest desserts. A Bittersweet Chocolate Icewine Truffle Cake is elevated when the bubbles carry the decadent chocolate to the forefront—magical. Imagine the perfect summer brunch of Vanilla-Infused Icewine Frenched Toast accompanied by Vidal Sparkling Icewine.

Icewine produced from the noble Riesling grape most clearly retains its vivid acidity and mineral notes, backed up by richer orange peel and citrus-fruit flavours. This style of sweet wine is best teamed with decadent foods such as seared foie gras, black chocolate crème brulée, or luscious cream sauces. The acidity cuts through the richness to create a new delicious textural profile.

A unique red Icewine is produced from Cabernet Franc grapes. This crimson version explodes with candied red berry flavours such as strawberry, cherry, and rhubarb. A Cabernet Franc Icewine has an underlying savoury aspect topped with a fresh, red-berry twist so it bodes well with a Cherry White Chocolate Mousse in Hazelnut Pastry or a simple dessert of Drunken Strawberries (fresh strawberries macerated in Cabernet Franc Icewine).

Icewines are also made from Gewürztraminer grapes, which provide their characteristic scented flavours of roses, lychee, dried figs, and soft spices. Pairing ginger-scented desserts and Gewürztraminer Icewine is worth the experience.

As the dinner table continues to change, we've never been freer to decide for ourselves what wines go with what foods. Roasted mutton has long been replaced with rack of lamb, aspic has lost favour, and the standard three-course meal has evolved into tasting menus. In fact, if a meal starts with grilled fish, followed by sorbet, and ends with soup, you'd be impressed with the ingenuity of the chef. The key therefore to evolving culinary fashion is to be decisive, clever, and insightful without being authoritarian.

For example, restaurants are now serving more dessert wines by the glass, revealing how Icewine can be served with more than just desserts. This culinary shift allows us to break old food and wine rules creatively and wisely, inspires resourcefulness, and provides an opportunity to experience the nuances of Icewine's influence at the dinner table. Icewine is not only an after-dinner wine but can also be a sweet alternative to dry Riesling.

Pairing is part of the entertainment, like a well-planned menu. The right combinations can stimulate your palate or soothe it, can turn sexy or impressive; properly chosen foods and wines can recreate memories or a particular theme; well-planned pairings allow for personal expression or celebrate an occasion or friend. Pairing Icewines with a variety of different foods can be one of the most creative aspects of a meal. For anyone who truly loves to dine rather than merely to eat, the words wine and food are linked. Whether it's savouring the intense aromas of a young fruity Icewine over a meal; recalling a culinary adventure at a memorable restaurant; drinking in the scents of fermenting wine in a barrel cellar; or concocting an anniversary dinner of Sweet Chévre Soufflé with Peach Sauce, Icewine is definitely a wine for the dinner table. Designing a meal around a special bottle of Icewine can be incredibly exciting because an appropriately chosen recipe or two often reveals something wonderful and new about Icewine.

Of course, combining wine and food is as subjective as enjoying art, literature, and architecture. The most sensible approach is to understand a few key guidelines for pairing and always remember that in the ritual of taste, there are no rules, only results to be validated for oneself. For the most harmonious dining, consider the following basic principles of Icewine and food compatibility.

You've heard it before; the sweetness of a dish should be less intense than that of the wine. Icewine can be served with something as simple as a pear or a savoury wedge of aged hard cheese. Icewine's flavours shine with a fresh fruit tart, poached fruit, or vanilla-laced grilled fruit. However, a dessert that is sweeter would undermine the wine, leaving a bitter taste, and the rich lusciousness of the Icewine may go unappreciated.

Icewine has a love affair with chocolate, which is probably the only food that rivals Icewine in complexity and nuance. Chocolate, like wine, has so many differ-

ent flavour characteristics: fruity, nutty, earthy, tobacco, floral, and vanilla. Rich milk chocolate brings out Icewine's vanilla flavours while the richness of a Bittersweet Chocolate Icewine Truffle Cake matches Icewine's succulent texture. As a dessert wine, Icewine has enough acidity to balance the sweetness in a dessert to create a luscious, yet delicate mouth feel out of the most luscious chocolate.

As in foods, there is an obvious difference in texture or firmness between different wines. Icewine has a very full texture and bold, rich flavours that make your palate sit up and take notice. For this reason delicate foods and light dishes are easily overwhelmed by Icewine's intensity. Therefore, we look to more robust-flavoured foods with equal texture and richness for harmony. For example, the full, silky texture of pâté on toast points mimics the richness of Icewine, and the bread contributes a toasty flavour that opens the door for an oak-aged Icewine.

Part of Icewine's magic is its broad spectrum of flavours, which pair well with many foods. Dishes that include flavours of apricot, peach, fig, vanilla, or pomegranate tend to emphasize the flavours of both the food and Icewine. For example, Roasted Leg of Lamb with Icewine Fig Compote works very well because of the similarity of flavours in the sauce that echo those in the wine.

Icewine can also provide contrasting flavours at the dining table. Sweet wines are a good contrast to savoury foods while matching textures beautifully. The classic

example of Icewine and foie gras works because of the contrast between the sweet and savoury. Foie gras' richness harmonizes with the Icewine's boldness, and the caramelization from searing echoes oak-aged Icewine's tones. Other savoury foods, such as succulent duck, rich terrines, and Seared Foie Gras with Icewine-Soaked Apricots, are terrific partners.

The aromas of Icewine have often been described as explosive. Lychee, honeyed peach, candied apricot, and ginger automatically conjure cravings for Asian cuisine. Perhaps this explains Asians' love affair with Icewine.

Acidity provides Icewine's versatility when it comes to amplifying the more subtle flavours of food. Pears become brilliant, apricots become succulent, and fruit flavours become clearer. The acidity provides a palate-cleansing contrast to rich or oily foods such as pâté and oysters.

For Icewines that spend time in oak before bottling, the wood itself contributes distinctive flavours of toast, caramel, and vanilla that match well with similar flavours in foods. This is one reason biscotti, the crisp double-baked cookie of Tuscany, pairs so well with Tuscany's sweet wine, vin santo, and why we've Canadianized the dessert with White Chocolate–Crowned Hazelnut Biscotti Pears. Dishes that include elements of toasted bread, cakes, or biscuits are all welcome flavours for oak-aged Icewines.

It makes sense to serve a glass of Icewine as an aperitif before dinner, perhaps with a few savoury hors d'oeuvres to create an immediate impact and to stimulate the appetite. Save the second half of the bottle to drink at the end of the meal, with or without dessert. Begin a meal with Sparkling Icewine and Truffled Cream of Cauliflower Soup then watch as the bubbles tame the thick creaminess of the soup while the elegant flavours play on your palate.

Icewines are magnificent with cheese, especially blue cheese such as Roquefort and Gorgonzola, hard and aged cheeses like Parmigiano-Reggiano and aged Gruyere, and some sheep's cheeses such as Pecorino. Other milder cheeses simply fade away against Icewine's dominant flavours. Nevertheless, foods made with cheese, such as a Sweet Chèvre Soufflé with Peach Sauce or authentic savoury cheesecakes can find no better partner than Icewine. Add the flavour of nuts to a cheese platter and you have an amazing end to a meal.

Icewine and food together create an embellished sensory experience to the dining table. If you find yourself confused and can't decide what to pair with what, don't panic. Feel free to experiment and know there are a lot of happy accidents waiting to happen.

RIESLING ICEWINE—THE APHRODISIAC

MARCEUS DELGADO
CHAMPION: CONCOUR MONDIALE DE SOMMELIER

The whole world thinks about the health benefits of red wine. The best example is the Asian world, where consumers even think that red wine is a perfect aphrodisiac.

With this fact in mind, I was travelling to Hong Kong in 1998. There, a journalist was quite negative about sweet wines, especially those from Germany. I did not know how to stop him and at a certain point I asked him for three minutes to tell him this story:

Everybody believes that red wine is an aphrodisiac; I am wondering why. Tannins are known to calm down the body, whereas acidity is linked to freshness and activity. Therefore a wine with some acidity would have a much more "refreshing" aspect.

On the other side, alcohol may have an effect on blood circulation but this effect slows down quickly, giving way to a feeling of relaxation and even tiredness. So a wine which has an aphrodisiac effect should have a lower degree of alcohol, just enough to stimulate but not too much, for prevention of tiring effects. Therefore an alcohol degree of around 10 Vol% in a white wine is much better than 14 Vol% in a red.

With the above mentioned paradigms, we are moving more and more towards white wine as an aphrodisiac. And the fact is confirmed by the Arabian physician Avincenna. He worked in the early Middle Ages on aromatherapy and used the flavours of peaches, apricots, and apples to stimulate aphrodisiac effects. And exactly these aromas you will find in Riesling!

Therefore, Riesling may be considered as an aphrodisiac, and there is an even stronger proof of it. Riesling has something even Viagra does not have: if it is a Kabinett or Spätlese, a Beerenauslese or Eiswein, there is plenty of residual sugar, giving energy. And one will need energy if all the above-mentioned aphrodisiac aspects work.

Therefore, Icewine is a perfect aphrodisiac, and you can even get it without a prescription.

Cooking with Icewine

RECIPES BY IZABELA KALABIS-SACCO AND LYNN OGRYZLO

Food and wine can each be delicious alone but it's incredibly exciting when they work together to make a better dish. Just as garlic, salt, and pepper add flavours and aromas, Icewine can work similar magic. Cooking with Icewine infuses both sweet and savoury foods with distinctive, soft, spicy, tropical fruits that become part of a dish's character.

Icewine can enhance a fruit compote, savoury sauce, basic stock, or a glaze. Add Icewine to marinades, dressings, and bastes; use it to deglaze a pan, soak fruit, or spike custard.

Chefs use Icewine as another flavour ingredient to play with, that is, according to the taste and aromatic characteristics of the dish. Adding a little Icewine to a sauce at the end of cooking will retain most the Icewine's aroma and flavour. If it's simmered a long time, as in a reduction, many of the distinctive flavour components concentrate to add an intense savouriness.

The high acidity in Icewine can tenderize meats while imparting flavour. Even fish and poultry gain tenderness and flavour from marinating.

When Icewines are flambéed, the sugar caramelizes and transforms into an earthy, sweet taste. Flambéing tree-ripened peaches with Icewine creates an exciting caramel essence. Since alcohol begins evaporating at a low boiling point, there is no alcohol left in most dishes cooked with wine.

Using Icewine as a fresh ingredient allows you to create some of the most delicious and simplest desserts in minutes. Try soaking sliced fresh apricots in Icewine and serving with a sprig of lemon balm and a little crème fraiche. Pour sparkling Icewine over field berries in a tall flute for a quick and elegant finale to any meal. Spike whipped cream with a few tablespoons of Icewine and spoon over fresh berries.

The following recipes include locally-harvested produce from the fields and orchards adjacent to Niagara's vineyards. You can source them and many more through www.NiagaraCulinaryTrail.com. This website offers harvest updates, culinary events, and details about many local growers. We thank them for providing the excellent produce that Niagara's chefs use to create dishes that so effectively complement Icewines.

Foie Gras with Granny Smith Apples and Blackcurrant Reduction

SERVES 4

An Oak-aged Icewine complements the foie gras because the toasted flavours from the barrels echo the earthy flavours of the seared foie gras. It's a classic combination of rich decadence.

Recipe by Inniskillin Resident Chef
Izabela Kalabis-Sacco

2 Granny Smith apples, core removed

2 Tbsp (30 mL) unsalted butter

2 Tbsp (30 mL) honey

2 Tbsp (30 mL) Vidal Icewine

1 cup (250 mL) good quality veal stock

2 Tbsp (30 mL) blackcurrant jelly

1 Tbsp (15 mL) Vidal Icewine

salt and freshly cracked black pepper

½ pound (225 g) whole foie gras, chilled

all-purpose flour for dredging

1 Tbsp (15 mL) unsalted butter

Cut each apple into 6 slices horizontally. In a large skillet over medium heat, melt butter with honey and Icewine. Add apple slices and sauté until the apple begins to soften, about 3 minutes. Set aside.

Pour veal stock into a small saucepan and bring to a boil. Lower heat to simmer and reduce stock by half. Add jelly and Icewine and reduce further until thickened, about 3 minutes. You may want to add a small splash of Icewine at this point, depending on sweetness of your sauce. Season to taste with salt and pepper. Keep warm while preparing foie gras.

Run a thin knife under hot water to warm it. Dry the knife and cut cold foie gras into 12 slices. Season with salt and pepper, and lightly dredge in flour. Cook foie gras slices in butter for about 30 seconds per side. The interior should remain very pink.

To serve, alternate slices of foie gras and apple and drizzle with blackcurrant sauce.

Serve with chilled Riesling or Oak-aged Vidal Icewine.

Seared Foie Gras with Icewine-Soaked Apricots

SERVES 4

Foie gras is the fattened liver of duck or goose. It can be a challenge to work with, but if you are looking for something sweet and savoury to launch an exquisite dinner, then this starter is well worth it.

10 ounces (250 g) foie gras, chilled

4 small, yellow-flesh potatoes, washed

1 tsp (5 mL) unsalted butter

1 tsp (5 mL) olive oil

¼ cup (60 mL) raw almonds

8 dried apricots, sliced in half horizontally

½ cup (125 mL) Vidal Icewine

½ cup (125 mL) seedless green grapes, washed and patted dry

salt and freshly ground black pepper

Run a thin knife under hot water to warm it. Dry the knife and cut foie gras into 16 slices. Season with salt and pepper, and refrigerate.

Slice potatoes into total of 16 thin slices, discarding the potato ends. Add butter and oil to a skillet and heat until butter melts. Add potatoes and cook until lightly browned, approximately 2 to 3 minutes. Season, turn over, and cook until done. Remove the potato slices from the pan and drain on a kitchen towel. Add the almonds to the skillet and cook for a few minutes until they become golden. Transfer to a cutting board and roughly chop the almonds.

Add the dried apricot halves and Icewine to the skillet. Bring to a simmer and cook for 15 minutes or until the Icewine has become quite syrupy and reduced by half. Slice half the grapes in half, leaving the remainder whole. Add all grapes to the skillet and cook for an additional 5 minutes. Remove the apricots and grapes and set aside.

Add the foie gras to the skillet and cook on high until golden brown, approximately 1 minute per side.

Lay 4 potato slices on each of 4 plates. Place dried apricot on each potato slice and top with foie gras. Sprinkle with chopped almonds and garnish with grapes around the edges. Drizzle with pan juices. Serve immediately.

Serve with chilled Vidal or Riesling Icewine.

Icewine and Thyme Grilled Fig Salad with Gorgonzola and Sherry Vinaigrette

SERVES 4

Although Icewine pairs beautifully with figs, adding a vinaigrette and gorgonzola makes a better match with sparkling Icewine; the effervescence takes the edge off the vinaigrette and provides a sublime textural contrast of fizz against the creamy gonzola.

Recipe by Inniskillin Resident Chef
Izabela Kalabis-Sacco

1 head of garlic

1 tsp (5 mL) olive oil

salt and freshly cracked black pepper

½ small fennel bulb

1 tsp (5 mL) olive oil

8 hazelnuts

VINAIGRETTE

1 Tbsp (15 mL) Vidal Icewine

2 Tbsp (30 mL) Sherry vinegar

5 Tbsp (75 mL) virgin olive oil

1 Tbsp (15 mL) hazelnut oil

pinch of thyme

salt and freshly cracked black pepper

1 Tbsp (15 mL) shallots, minced

1 clove roasted garlic

4 ounces (100 g) Gorgonzola cheese

2 Tbsp (30 mL) unsalted butter

2 Tbsp (30 mL) Vidal Icewine

½ tsp (2.5 mL) fennel seeds, crushed

1 tsp (5 mL) fresh thyme, chopped

salt and freshly cracked black pepper

4 ripe figs

4 cups (1 L) mixed greens—watercress, arugula, endive, mizuna, red oak, etc.

Preheat oven to 350°F (180°C). Slice the top off an entire head of garlic to expose the tips of the cloves. Place on large piece of foil, drizzle with olive oil, and season with salt and pepper. Wrap in foil and roast in oven for 30–40 minutes or until soft.

Meanwhile, remove and discard the outer layers of fennel bulb and remove core. Julienne fennel and toss with olive oil. Place in a small roasting pan and roast for 35 minutes. Remove and allow to cool.

Meanwhile, rub skins off the hazelnuts with your fingers and place on a small baking sheet. Bake for 5 minutes or until lightly browned, being careful not to burn them. Allow to cool and chop coarsely.

Mash the clove of roasted garlic with a fork. Combine vinaigrette ingredients in a medium bowl. Whisk and season to taste. Set aside.

Slice the Gorgonzola into 4 chunks and set aside. Heat the butter with Icewine, fennel seeds, thyme, salt, and pepper in a small skillet. Add the figs and sauté for 2 to 3 minutes or until soft. Remove from skillet and, leaving base attached, cut the figs vertically into quarters. Place a piece of gorgonzola in centre of each fig.

Toss greens and fennel in dressing and arrange on 4 individual plates. Place a fig on top of each salad and sprinkle with toasted hazelnuts.

Serve with chilled Riesling or Sparkling Vidal Icewine.

Truffled Cream of Cauliflower Soup

SERVES 6

The weight of the dish is an important consideration when pairing a wine. This savoury soup is full and luscious and pairs well with an Oak-aged Icewine.

3 Tbsp (45 mL) extra virgin olive oil

3 Tbsp (45 mL) unsalted butter

4 slices pancetta, chopped

1 medium onion, chopped

1 head cauliflower, washed and roughly chopped

4 cups (1 L) chicken stock

1 truffle, sliced very thinly with a truffle shaver or mandolin

4 Tbsp (60 mL) all-purpose flour

1 cup (250 mL) light cream

salt and freshly ground white pepper

4 drops truffle oil

Heat the oil and butter in a stock pot and cook the pancetta until it is crisp. Add the onion and cauliflower and cook for 10 minutes. Add the stock and half the truffle slices, bring to a boil and simmer for an additional 10 minutes. Remove from heat and cool enough to handle. Purée in a blender. Return soup to pot and heat over medium-low heat.

Mix the flour and cream until very smooth. Add to the soup very slowly, stirring constantly. Simmer for 6 to 8 minutes and season to taste with salt and pepper.

Ladle soup into 6 individual soup bowls and garnish with remaining truffle slices. Drizzle with a few drops of truffle oil and serve warm.

Serve with chilled Oak-aged Vidal or Sparkling Icewine.

Vineyard Leg of Lamb with Icewine Fig Compote

SERVES 4

An Icewine-infused fig compote accompanies the savoury sweetness of the roasted garlic. Icewine's body stands up to lamb exquisitely.

1 4 lb (1.81 kg) leg of lamb

2 cloves garlic, slivered

½ cup (125 mL) Vidal Icewine

1 tsp (5 mL) dried rosemary

1 tsp (5 mL) salt

2 tsp (10 mL) freshly ground black pepper

1 Tbsp (15 mL) sugar

½ cup (125 mL) Vidal Icewine

grated zest of half a lemon

6 fresh figs, peeled, stemmed, and quartered

½ vanilla bean

¼ tsp (1.25 mL) fennel seeds

1 cinnamon stick, about 2 inches long

2 whole cloves

1 Tbsp (15 mL) lemon juice

Using a sharp, pointed knife, make small slits all over the leg of lamb and insert the garlic slivers. Soak a cheesecloth or tea towel in the Icewine and lay it over the lamb. Cover with plastic and marinate, refrigerated, for 4 hours or overnight.

Preheat oven to 450°F (230°C). Mix rosemary, salt, and pepper in a small bowl. Unwrap lamb and place fat side up on a rack in a roasting pan. Press rosemary mixture over lamb, covering evenly. Roast for 30 minutes. Reduce heat to 350°F (180°C). Continue to roast for an hour or until desired doneness. A meat thermometer inserted into the thickest part of the leg should read 135–140°F (55–60°C) for rare; 140–145°F (60–65°C) for medium rare; and 150–155°F (65–70°C) for medium.

Meanwhile, in a small saucepan, combine the sugar and Icewine. Slowly bring to a boil, stirring until sugar is dissolved. Remove from the heat and add lemon zest and figs. Tie the vanilla bean, fennel seeds, cinnamon stick, and cloves in a piece of cheesecloth and add to the pan. Let stand for 10 minutes.

Bring to a boil and reduce heat to medium. Simmer for 15 minutes or until most of the liquid has evaporated. Add lemon juice and stir. Remove the cheesecloth and allow compote to cool.

Remove roast from oven and let stand 10 minutes before carving. Serve with Icewine fig compote on the side.

Serve with chilled Oak-aged Vidal Icewine.

Shredded Duck Breast Prosciutto and Mango Salad

SERVES 6

The generous character of the duck breast prosciutto adds richness to a fresh, fruity salad. The combination pairs naturally with the Icewine used in the dressing.

1 large, firm mango, peeled and julienned

1 cucumber, peeled, seeded, and julienned

2 thick carrots, peeled and julienned

4 spring onions, cut in 4-inch lengths and very thinly sliced lengthways

2-inch piece fresh ginger, peeled and julienned

½ long red chili, seeded and shredded

small bunch fresh cilantro, cleaned and roughly chopped

½ small duck breast prosciutto, julienned

DRESSING

2 Tbsp (30 mL) Vidal Icewine

2 Tbsp (30 mL) Thai fish sauce

1 Tbsp (15 mL) lime juice

4 tsp (20 mL) tamarind paste

In a large bowl combine mango, cucumber, carrots, spring onions, fresh ginger, chili, and cilantro. Toss well.

In a small bowl, whisk the Icewine, fish sauce, lime juice, and tamarind paste until well combined. Pour the dressing over the salad and toss well. Arrange salad on each of 6 individual salad plates and top with prosciutto.

Serve with chilled Vidal or Riesling Icewine.

Icewine-Marinated Pork Medallions with Corn-Crusted Onion Rings

SERVES 4

Searing and roasting concentrates the flavours of pork where the Icewine marinade has penetrated, giving a sweet caramelized taste to the crusty surface. The hot and spicy flavours play off the sweet, caramelized Icewine.

6 dried red chilies

3 Tbsp (45 mL) hot water

2 garlic cloves, minced

1 tsp (5 mL) dried sage

4 Tbsp (60 mL) Vidal Icewine

4 Tbsp (60 mL) extra virgin olive oil

1 10-ounce (250 g) pork tenderloin

½ cup (125 mL) whole milk

1 egg, beaten

1 onion, sliced into rings

½ cup (125 mL) coarse cornmeal

1 tsp (5 mL) red chili flakes, dried

1 tsp (5 mL) dried parsley

salt and freshly cracked black pepper

Canola oil, for deep-frying

Place the chilies in a bowl, cover with hot water, and let soak for 20 to 30 minutes. Reserving the water, drain. Using a food processor, process the chilies into a paste with the garlic, sage, Icewine, and oil. Rub the chili paste all over the pork tenderloin (add a little reserved soaking water, if needed) and let marinate overnight.

Whisk the milk and egg together. Separate the onion into rings and soak in the milk mixture for 30 minutes.

Heat oven to 350°F (160°C). Heat a cast-iron grill pan. Season the tenderloin with salt and pepper and sear it on the stove for about 2 minutes on each side. Transfer pan to oven and bake for 20 minutes for medium, adapting time according to how rare or well-done you like your pork. Remove from oven and let stand for 5 minutes.

Meanwhile mix the cornmeal, chili, and parsley together, and season with salt and pepper. Heat the canola oil to 325–350°F (150–180°C).

Remove a few onion rings from the milk mixture and dip each into the cornmeal mixture, coating thoroughly. Fry in batches for 2 to 4 minutes, or until lightly browned and crisp. Do not overcrowd the pan. Remove the onion rings from the pan with a slotted spoon and drain on paper towels.

To serve, slice tenderloin on a diagonal, into 12 equal slices. Place 3 on each of 4 individual dinner plates and top with onion rings.

Serve with chilled Oak-aged Vidal or Riesling Icewine.

Apple-Grape Tart with Icewine Crust

MAKES 1 TART

The simplicity of this harvest tart provides a light, flavourful end to a meal. Because apples and grapes are picked at the same time of year, they're naturally pleasing partners on the palate.

Recipe by Inniskillin Resident Chef
Izabela Kalabis-Sacco

PASTRY

2 cups (500 mL) all-purpose flour, sifted

Pinch of salt

1 cup (250 mL) cold, unsalted butter, cut into large pieces

5 Tbsp (75 mL) icing sugar, sifted

2 Tbsp (30 mL) Vidal Icewine

1 egg

FILLING

1 pound (450 g) Golden Delicious or Granny Smith apples

6 Tbsp (90 mL) unsalted butter

4 Tbsp (60 mL) sugar

1 vanilla bean, split lengthwise

4 Tbsp (60 mL) Vidal Icewine

5 Tbsp (75 mL) apricot jam

⅓ pound (150 g) seedless red or green grapes

Sift flour and salt in a large bowl. Add butter and work lightly and quickly with pastry cutter until mixture resembles coarse meal. Mix together icing sugar, Icewine, and egg and add it to the flour mixture. Knead lightly until dough holds together. On a clean surface knead to blend in butter. Do not overwork. Wrap in wax paper and chill for 30 minutes or overnight.

Peel and core apples and slice thinly. Melt butter in large skillet over moderate heat and add sugar. Stir and cook 2 to 3 minutes, stirring constantly. Using a sharp knife, scrape seeds from inside vanilla bean into skillet, discarding bean pod. Add apples and stir well to coat with mixture, continuing to cook for about 3 minutes. When apples begin to soften, add Icewine, stir, and remove from heat. Set aside to cool.

Preheat oven to 425°F (220°C). Remove dough from refrigerator and roll on a clean, floured surface. Line a 9-inch tart tin with pastry. Brush half the apricot jam in an even layer on base of uncooked tart. Arrange apple slices in a wheel pattern, overlapping them slightly, over the base of the tart. Place grapes in centre of tart.

Bake tart in preheated oven for 20 minutes. Remove from oven and brush remaining glaze on top. Serve warm or at room temperature.

Serve with chilled Vidal or Riesling Icewine.

Bittersweet Chocolate Icewine Truffle Cake

MAKES 1 LOAF CAKE

Chocolate desserts as over-the-top rich as this one can be difficult wine partners, but Icewine's acidity and intensity cut through the richness.

Recipe by Inniskillin Resident Chef Izabela Kalabis-Sacco

8.5 ounces (230 g) bittersweet chocolate, chopped coarsely

¾ cup (180 mL) plain butter cookies (arrowroot or short-bread style)

4 egg yolks

⅓ cup (80 mL) whole milk

⅓ cup (80 mL) Vidal Icewine

¾ cup (180 mL) unsalted butter, softened

¾ cup (180 mL) ground almonds

5 ounces (140 g) bittersweet chocolate, chopped coarsely

2 Tbsp (30 mL) whipping cream

Melt chocolate in a bowl over a simmering pot of water. Remove from heat and let cool. Meanwhile, chop cookies in a food processor until reduced to a fine powder. Set aside. Add egg yolks one by one to chocolate, whisking vigorously after each addition.

In a saucepan over medium-high heat, bring milk to a boil. Slowly drizzle the hot milk into the chocolate mixture, whisking constantly to avoid scrambling the yolks. When all milk has been incorporated, pour chocolate mixture into a saucepan and place over medium heat. Stirring constantly with a wooden spoon, cook until it thickens, about 6 minutes. Do not boil. Remove from heat, let cool, and whisk in Icewine, butter, cookie powder, and ground almonds. Pour mixture into loaf pan. Refrigerate until set.

To unmould, dip loaf pan briefly in a large container filled with hot water, then quickly tip upside down to release cake.

For the icing, melt chocolate in a bowl over a simmering pot of water. When melted, remove from heat and add cream. Whisk and carefully pour on top of cake.

Serve with chilled Cabernet Franc Icewine.

Bosc Pear Mousse with Chocolate Biscuit and Caramel Sauce

SERVES 6

Orchard fruits such as pear call for wines with similarly fruity character, especially when the fruit is at its peak of ripeness; Icewines are naturals. Each of the recipe steps can be prepared the day before for an easy-to-assemble dessert.

Recipe by Inniskillin Resident Chef
Izabela Kalabis-Sacco

CHOCOLATE BISCUIT
6 ounces (170 g) bittersweet chocolate, coarsely chopped
1 cup (250 mL) unsalted butter
5 eggs, separated
3 Tbsp (45 mL) sugar
1 Tbsp (15 mL) all-purpose flour

PEAR MOUSSE
1 cup (250 mL) whole milk
½ cup (125 mL) heavy cream
1 vanilla bean, split lengthwise
3 large egg yolks
½ cup (125 mL) sugar
½ cup (125 mL) heavy cream
4 cups (1 L) water
⅔ cup (160 mL) sugar
juice of 1 lemon
3 pounds (1.8 kg) Bosc pears
3 Tbsp (45 mL) sugar
½ cup (125 mL) whipping cream,
  whipped

CARAMEL SAUCE
½ cup (125 mL) sugar
¼ cup (60 mL) water
¼ cup (60 mL) heavy cream

For the biscuit, butter a 10- × 15-inch (25 cm × 35 cm) baking sheet. Line bottom with parchment paper. Preheat oven to 350°F (180°C).

Melt chocolate with butter in a bowl over simmering water. Let cool to lukewarm. Beat egg yolks with sugar. Add melted chocolate and flour, and mix well. Beat egg whites until soft peaks form and gently fold into chocolate mixture. Pour mixture into a thin layer in prepared pan, and bake 25 to 30 minutes or until slightly springy on top. Remove from oven and let cool completely. Carefully peel off parchment.

Make mousse by combining milk and cream in a saucepan. Using the tip of a sharp knife, scrape the seeds from half the vanilla bean into the milk mixture. Cook over medium heat until bubbles form around the edges of the pan, about 5 minutes.

Meanwhile, combine the egg yolks, sugar, and cream in a bowl and whisk until mixture is smooth and the sugar begins to dissolve.

Very slowly, pour approximately ¼ cup (60 mL) of the hot milk mixture into the yolk mixture, whisking vigorously. Continue adding more milk slowly until half the milk is used. Pour the milk/yolk mixture into the saucepan with the remaining hot milk and cook over low heat, stirring constantly with a wooden spoon until it is thick enough to coat the back of the spoon, approximately 6 minutes. Remove from heat and set aside to cool.

In a saucepan over high heat, combine water, sugar, lemon juice, and seeds scraped from the remaining half of vanilla bean. Peel, core, and halve pears. Reduce the heat to a simmer and poach pears in the sugar syrup until tender, approximately 6 to 8 minutes.

Remove 3 pear halves, dice finely, and place in strainer to drain. Cool the remaining pears enough to purée them with sugar. Stir pear purée into

custard along with diced pears. Refrigerate until it starts to set. Fold the whipped cream into pear mousse. Refrigerate again to set completely.

In a small saucepan over high heat, boil sugar and water together until mixture begins to turn a deep golden colour. Remove from heat and allow bubbles to subside. Standing back, carefully and slowly add cream as mixture may bubble vigorously. Return to low heat until caramel is smooth, stirring constantly. Allow to cool.

When ready to serve, peel the parchment from the chocolate biscuit and cut into squares or desired shape. Top with a scoop of pear mousse and drizzle with caramel sauce.

Serve with chilled Riesling or Oak-aged Vidal Icewine.

Champagne Cake with Caramelized Orange Sauce

MAKES 6 INDIVIDUAL CAKES

The silky texture of the champagne filling mimics the luscious mouth feel of Icewine while the sauce does a particularly good job of bringing out Icewine's tangerine notes. It's an exquisite combination.

Recipe by Inniskillin Resident Chef
Izabela Kalabis-Sacco

CAKE
6 eggs, room temperature
¾ cup (180 mL) sugar
¾ cup (180 mL) all-purpose flour
⅓ cup (80 mL) unsweetened cocoa
3 Tbsp (45 mL) unsalted butter, melted and slightly cooled

CHAMPAGNE FILLING
2 gelatin packets
1 vanilla bean, split lengthwise
1 cup (250 mL) sparkling wine
4 eggs, separated
4 Tbsp (60 mL) sugar
1 cup (250 mL) whipping cream
1 Tbsp (15 mL) sugar
4 Tbsp (60 mL) orange liqueur

ORANGE SAUCE
⅓ cup (80 mL) sugar
juice of ½ lemon
1 cup (250 mL) orange juice

Preheat oven to 375°F (190°C) and line two 10- × 15-inch (25 cm × 35 cm) baking sheets with parchment paper.

Using an electric mixer, beat eggs with sugar on low speed for 5 minutes. Increase speed to medium and beat for another 10 minutes. Turn mixer off. Sift flour and cocoa together, and gently fold into egg mixture. Fold in melted butter. Spread a thin layer of batter onto each baking sheet and bake for 10 to 12 minutes or until set. Take sheets of cake out of oven, turn out of pans, and let cool.

Soften gelatin according to package instructions. Scrape vanilla seeds from bean using the tip of a sharp knife and add to sparkling wine in a saucepan over medium-high heat. Meanwhile, using a whisk, beat egg yolks with sugar. When bubbles appear around the edge of the wine, pour it very slowly into the egg mixture, whisking vigorously the entire time. Be careful not to scramble the eggs. Pour the egg mixture back into the saucepan and place it over low heat. Continue whisking until mixture thickens, approximately 6 minutes. Do not let boil. Remove from heat and add gelatin to the hot mixture. Whisk until it dissolves.

Beat cream until soft peaks form. In another bowl, beat egg whites until soft peaks form, add sugar, and continue beating for another minute. Gently fold whipped cream and egg whites into custard. Chill until mixture thickens, about 3 hours.

Cut cake layers into 24 pieces. Place a piece of cake on each of 6 dessert plates. Using a pastry brush, moisten the cake with a bit of orange liqueur. Spoon a heaping tablespoon of filling on cake, cover with another piece of cake, moisten with liqueur again, spoon another dollop of filling on top, and continue until you have used all cake pieces and filling. Refrigerate until ready to serve.

In a saucepan over high heat, melt sugar and lemon juice until a deep caramel colour. Take off heat, and, standing back, add orange juice gradually as the caramel may bubble vigorously. Stir well and let cool. Drizzle orange sauce over cake and serve immediately.

Serve with chilled Sparkling Icewine.

Cherry White Chocolate Mousse Tart with Hazelnut Pastry

MAKES ONE 9-INCH TART

A vibrant and delicate tart with appealing vanilla, cherry, and toasty notes marries beautifully with Icewine.

Recipe by Inniskillin Resident Chef
Izabela Kalabis-Sacco

PASTRY

½ cup (125 mL) all-purpose flour

pinch of salt

¼ cup (60 mL) hazelnuts, ground

2 Tbsp (30 mL) sugar

¼ cup (60 mL) unsalted butter, chilled

1 egg yolk

1 tsp (5 mL) water

MOUSSE

⅔ cup (160 mL) white chocolate, coarsely chopped

2 egg yolks

1 cup (250 mL) whipping cream

½ cup (125 mL) apricot marmalade

1 Tbsp (15 mL) water

about 30 dark, sweet cherries

In a large bowl, whisk flour, salt, hazelnuts, and sugar together. Add butter and work in with pastry cutter. Mix yolk and water together and add to the flour mixture. Work with fingers until dough just holds together. Wrap in wax paper and chill 20 minutes.

Melt chocolate in a bowl set over a simmering pot of water. Whisk egg yolks in a small bowl set over hot water until thick and frothy. Remove from heat, whisk in chocolate, and chill. Whip cream until soft peaks form, then fold into chocolate mixture. Refrigerate until set, about 1 hour.

Preheat oven to 375°F (190°C). On floured surface roll out dough to line a 9-inch (23 cm) tart tin. Prick bottom of pastry with fork, line with parchment paper, and cover paper with dried beans. Bake for 15 to 18 minutes. Remove from oven and let cool to room temperature.

Meanwhile, melt marmalade and water over low heat.

Fill tart shell with mousse. Arrange cherries on top of tart in the shape of a grape cluster and brush cherries with apricot glaze. Chill until ready to serve.

Serve with chilled Cabernet Franc Icewine.

White Chocolate–Crowned Hazelnut Biscotti Pears

SERVES 6

The velvety texture of white chocolate and crunchy biscotti coat a luscious pear. The exotic surprise inside of Icewine-laced mascarpone cheese finishes it exquisitely.

½ cup (125 mL) unsalted butter, room temperature

1 cup (250 mL) sugar

2 eggs

1 tsp (5 mL) pure vanilla extract

1 tsp (5 mL) orange zest

2 cups (500 mL) all-purpose flour

1 ½ tsp (7.5 mL) baking powder

pinch of salt

1 cup (250 mL) hazelnuts, finely chopped

6 Bosc pears

⅓ cup (80 mL) mascarpone cheese

1 Tbsp (15 mL) Vidal Icewine

1 cup (250 mL) or more of coarse sugar for coating

4 ounces (100 g) white chocolate

4 tsp (20 mL) whipping cream

To make biscotti dough, beat butter, sugar, and eggs until light and fluffy. Add vanilla and orange zest, and continue beating until creamy. Whisk flour, baking powder, and salt together. Add to butter mixture and mix until well incorporated. Add chopped hazelnuts and mix by hand until just combined. Set aside.

Slice bottom of pears so they sit upright. With a paring knife, remove core from the bottom, leaving pears intact. Whisk mascarpone with Icewine and divide between pear cavities. Sit pears upright on baking sheet and press biscotti dough over the entire pear to seal it. Coat each pear with raw sugar and place on a baking sheet.

Bake at 325°F (160°C) for 35 to 40 minutes or until lightly browned. Allow to cool. Meanwhile, melt the white chocolate in a bowl over a simmering pot of hot water. When chocolate is completely melted, add whipping cream and whisk until smooth. Spoon white chocolate on top of the pear and allow it to run down the sides. Serve at room temperature.

Serve with chilled Oak-aged Vidal or Sparkling Icewine.

Icewine Custard with Sugared Pecans

*Icewine partners with pear and custard to provide a pastry-rich
complexity and a luxurious finish.*

SERVES 4

4 tsp (20 mL) Vidal Icewine
5 large egg yolks
1 large whole egg
1 cup (250 mL) pure maple syrup
4 tsp (20 mL) unsalted butter
½ cup (125 mL) pecan halves
4 tsp (20 mL) sugar
pinch of salt
Boiling water

Preheat the oven to 325°F (160°C). Spoon 1 tsp (5 mL) Icewine into each of 4 ramekins, swirling to coat the bottoms. Arrange the ramekins in a roasting pan.

In a large bowl, whisk the yolks with the whole egg until blended. Whisk in the maple syrup. Pour the mixture into the ramekins. Carefully pour enough very hot water into the roasting pan to reach halfway up the sides of the ramekins. Cover the pan with foil and bake for about 55 minutes, or until the custards are just set. Remove from oven.

Using tongs, immediately remove the ramekins from the hot water and let cool to room temperature. Refrigerate the custards for at least 6 hours or overnight.

Meanwhile, in a large skillet, melt the butter. Add the pecans and stir to coat with the butter. Cook over moderate heat until lightly browned, about 5 minutes. Put the sugar in a plastic bowl with a lid. Add pecans, attach the lid, and gently shake to coat the pecans. Transfer the nuts to a baking sheet, shaking off any excess sugar. Sprinkle lightly with salt. Let cool.

Carefully run a knife around the edge of each ramekin to separate the custard from the ramekin. Dip each ramekin in a bowl of boiling water for a minute, then quickly invert the custard onto a plate. Garnish with sugared pecans and serve.

Serve with Vidal or Riesling Icewine.

Vanilla-Infused Icewine Frenched Toast

SERVES 4

Icewine's tropical flavours and honey-like essence add a lovely decadence to a favourite lazy-morning breakfast. The bread's toasted flavour opens the door for an Oak-aged Icewine.

1 egg, lightly beaten

2 egg whites

3 Tbsp (45 mL) Vidal Icewine

1 Tbsp (15 mL) sugar

1 vanilla bean, split lengthwise

½ cup (125 mL) whole milk

1 Tbsp (15 mL) unsalted butter

8 thick slices baguette, cut on a diagonal

1 cup (250 mL) pure maple syrup

½ cup (125 mL) Vidal Icewine

icing sugar for dusting

Place the egg, egg whites, Icewine, and sugar in a bowl and whisk to combine. Using the tip of a sharp knife, scrape the seeds from the vanilla bean into the egg mixture. Add milk and whisk until frothy.

Heat a large skillet over medium heat and melt butter. Dip a few pieces of bread into the egg mixture, soaking both sides well, and place in the skillet. Cook for 2 minutes on each side or until lightly golden. Repeat with the remaining bread.

Mix maple syrup with Icewine. Serve French toast dusted with icing sugar and drizzled with maple/Icewine mixture.

Serve with chilled Oak-aged Vidal or Sparkling Icewine.

Icewine-Soaked Figs on Hazelnut Crust with White Chocolate Mousse, Icewine Sabayon, and Raspberry Coulis

SERVES 4

The silky richness of desserts like this one can be challenging to partner with most wines, but Icewine matches this dessert's luscious elements and satiny mouth feel. Each of the recipe steps can be prepared the day before for an easy-to-assemble dessert.

Recipe by Inniskillin Resident Chef Izabela Kalabis-Sacco

HAZELNUT CRUST
3 egg whites

1 Tbsp (15 mL) sugar

½ cup (125 mL) hazelnuts, ground

½ cup (125 mL) icing sugar

1 Tbsp (15 mL) all-purpose flour, sifted

WHITE CHOCOLATE MOUSSE
3 eggs, separated

½ cup (125 mL) icing sugar

4 ounces (100 g) white chocolate, chopped or broken into small pieces

2 Tbsp (30 mL) unsalted butter

1 cup (250 mL) whipping cream

FIGS
1 Tbsp (15 mL) unsalted butter

4 ripe figs

½ cup (125 mL) Vidal Icewine

SABAYON
2 egg yolks

1 Tbsp (15 mL) sugar

¼ cup (60 mL) Vidal Icewine

RASPBERRY COULIS
1 cup (250 mL) fresh raspberries

2 Tbsp (30 mL) icing sugar

Preheat oven to 300°F (150°C). Line a baking sheet with parchment paper. Use a pencil to draw eight 3-inch circles on it.

Beat egg whites until soft peaks form. Add sugar, beat for another minute. Whisk together ground hazelnuts, icing sugar, and flour. Gently fold into egg whites. Using a piping bag, pipe out the 8 circles. Bake for about 30 minutes or until dry. Remove from oven and allow to cool.

Combine the egg yolks and icing sugar in a heatproof mixing bowl. Beat with an electric mixer on high speed until light yellow, about 5 minutes. Place bowl over a saucepan of simmering water. Heat, whisking constantly, until quite thick, about 4 to 5 minutes. Set aside.

Melt the chocolate and butter in a bowl over a saucepan of simmering water, stirring constantly until smooth. Remove from heat and let cool to room temperature. Add the chocolate to the egg mixture, stirring until smooth. Let cool to room temperature.

Meanwhile, in a chilled bowl beat the cream until quite stiff. Wash and dry beaters. In a separate bowl beat egg whites until stiff peaks form. Fold the egg whites into the chocolate mixture, then gently fold in the whipped cream. Refrigerate for an hour or until set.

Melt butter in pan large enough to hold figs. Add figs and cook over moderate heat for 1 minute, turning figs gently. Add Icewine and continue cooking until wine is almost evaporated and figs are slightly caramelized, about 5 minutes. Cut a deep cross in the top of each fig three-quarters of the way down and set aside.

To make the sabayon, whisk egg yolks, sugar, and Icewine in a bowl placed

over a saucepan of simmering water until thick, approximately 5 minutes.

Purée raspberries in food processor or food mill and pass through sieve to remove seeds. Add the sugar and stir well.

To assemble, place a hazelnut crust on each of 4 dessert plates. Spoon white chocolate mousse on top, press another hazelnut crust on top of mousse, and press slightly. Spoon more mousse on hazelnut crust and top with a fig. Spread open the fig and drizzle sabayon into the centre. Surround dessert with raspberry sauce.

Serve with chilled Vidal, Riesling, or Cabernet Franc Icewine.

Peaches with Raspberry-Icewine Purée

SERVES 4

Sweetness in food, like acidity, needs to be balanced by the accompanying wine. It sounds simple enough, and in the case of this fruit dish, it is. The Icewine is slightly sweeter than the peaches and raspberry purée, creating a brilliance of flavour.

1 cup (250 mL) raspberries

3 Tbsp (45 mL) Cabernet Franc Icewine

6 ripe peaches

mint sprigs for garnish

In a blender at medium speed, blend raspberries and Icewine until smooth. Strain to remove seeds if desired. Chill until ready to use.

Plunge peaches into boiling water for 10 seconds and peel the skins. Halve each peach, removing and discarding pits. Chill until ready to use.

Slice the bottom of 4 peaches so they sit well on a plate. Place 2 more peach halves on top and spoon raspberry Icewine sauce over the top. Garnish with mint sprigs and serve immediately.

Serve with chilled Cabernet Franc Icewine.

Crispy Pears with Icewine Sorbet

Pear sorbet and sparkling wine are a classic; however, Sparkling Icewine brings plenty of concentrated fruit complexity to add pizzazz to the elegant components.

SORBET
4 pears, Bartlett or Bosc
4 cups (1 L) water
¼ cup (60 mL) sugar
1 vanilla bean, split lengthwise

CRISPY PEARS
2 pears, Bartlett or Bosc
juice of 1 lemon
½ cup (125 mL) Icewine
ground hazelnuts for garnish

Peel and core pears. In a large saucepan, boil the water and sugar until thick and syrupy, about 5 minutes. With the edge of a sharp knife, scrape the seeds from the vanilla bean into the syrup. Add the vanilla bean and pears and cook over medium heat until the pears are tender, approximately 1 hour. Reserving the syrup, remove the pears and discard the vanilla bean. Purée pears in a blender or food processor. Combine the pear purée and reserved syrup, Pour into an ice cream machine and follow the manufacturer's directions to make sorbet.

To make the crispy pears, cut the pears into paper-thin slices lengthwise, discarding the ends, for a total of 24 slices. Squeeze lemon juice over them to prevent discoloration. Soak in Icewine for 20 minutes. Transfer to a cooling rack and allow to dry for 48 hours.

To serve, place 2 scoops of Icewine sorbet into each of the 6 dessert bowls. Place a pear slice into each mound vertically. Drizzle with additional Icewine and garnish with chopped hazelnuts.

Served with a chilled glass of Sparkling Icewine.

Ricotta Crepes with Drunken Strawberries

SERVES 6

Traditionally, eggs and cheese coat the mouth and allow very little wine flavour to show. Cabernet Franc Icewine's high acidity penetrates the cheese and provides the fruitiness to match the strawberries.

DRUNKEN STRAWBERRIES

1 cup (250 mL) fresh strawberries, washed, hulled, and diced

½ cup (125 mL) Cabernet Franc Icewine

1 tsp (5 mL) honey

CREPES

2 eggs

½ cup (125 mL) whole milk

½ cup (125 mL) water

¾ cup (175 mL) all-purpose flour

1 tsp (5 mL) sugar

1 Tbsp (15 mL) canola oil

FILLING

1 cup (250 mL) ricotta cheese

½ cup (125 mL) cream cheese

2 Tbsp (30 mL) Vidal Icewine

1 tsp (5 mL) pure vanilla extract

1 Tbsp (15 mL) unsalted butter, melted

mint sprigs for garnish

Place strawberries in a bowl. In another bowl, whisk together the Icewine and honey. Pour over strawberries and allow to macerate for an hour.

Whisk together eggs, milk, and water. In another bowl, mix together flour and sugar. Add to milk mixture and whisk until batter is smooth. Let sit for 30 minutes.

Using the 1 tablespoon (15 mL) of oil, lightly oil the bottom of a large skillet, wiping away any excess with a paper towel. Place skillet over medium heat and pour in 2 tablespoons (30 mL) of batter. Immediately tilt the pan to coat the bottom evenly with a thin layer of batter. Cook for approximately 30 seconds or until the top looks dry. Turn crepe and continue to cook for another 30 seconds. Remove from pan. Continue making crepes until you have 12 crepes, layered between sheets of waxed paper to keep them separate.

Preheat oven to 400°F (200°C). Lightly oil a large baking dish.

In a medium bowl, combine ricotta cheese, cream cheese, Icewine, and vanilla. Mix well. Spoon about 2 tablespoons (15 mL) of ricotta filling onto the centre of each crepe. Fold the crepe in half and press to spread filling, fold in half again to form a triangle. Place crepes in the prepared baking dish and brush lightly with melted butter. Bake for 10 to 15 minutes or until heated through.

To serve, place 2 crepes on each of 6 small plates and top with drunken strawberries and a sprig of fresh mint.

Serve with chilled Cabernet Franc Icewine.

Summer Berries with Chilled Icewine Cream

SERVES 4

Icewine's natural fruit and berry character pairs beautifully with this dessert. The silky texture of the cream mimics Icewine's luscious flavours while Icewine's acidity cuts the dessert's richness.

Recipe by Inniskillin Resident Chef
Izabela Kalabis-Sacco

2 cups (500 mL) mixed seasonal berries such as strawberries, blueberries, raspberries, blackberries, and currants, washed and sliced if needed

⅓ cup (80 mL) Vidal Icewine

ICEWINE CREAM
3 egg yolks
2 Tbsp (30 mL) sugar
½ cup (125 mL) Vidal Icewine
½ cup (125 mL) whipping cream
Fresh mint or lavender for garnish

Pour Icewine over berries and refrigerate for an hour.

In a small saucepan over low heat, whisk together egg yolks, sugar, and Icewine. Whisk until thickened, about 5 to 6 minutes. Remove from heat and continue to whisk for another minute or until slightly cooled. Chill mixture for 20 minutes. Whip cream until soft peaks form and fold into cooled egg mixture. Chill for at least 30 minutes.

Divide berries and juice between 4 individual bowls or large wine glasses. Top with a large spoonful of Icewine cream and garnish with mint or lavender.

Serve with chilled Riesling or Vidal Icewine.

Sweet Chèvre Soufflé with Peach Sauce

SERVES 4

This light, delicious soufflé, with the unmistakable tang of goat's cheese, is perfect for a summer breakfast or a light treat to end any meal.

Recipe by Inniskillin Resident Chef
Izabela Kalabis-Sacco

SOUFFLÉ
Unsalted butter and sugar for ramekins
3 ½ ounces (89 g) creamy goat's cheese
4 Tbsp (60 mL) sugar
2 whole eggs, separated
½ tsp (2.5 mL) orange zest
1 egg white

PEACH SAUCE
2 tree-ripened peaches
¼ cup (60 mL) Vidal Icewine
3 Tbsp (45 mL) sugar
1 vanilla bean, split lengthwise
cinnamon stick
few whole cloves
½ tsp (2.5 mL) lemon juice
4 peach slices for garnish
lime zest for garnish

Prepare 4 ramekins by buttering each one well and sprinkling each with sugar. Preheat oven to 375°F (190°C).

Using an electric mixer, beat goat's cheese. Add 2 tablespoons sugar and mix well. Add egg yolks and orange zest to cheese mixture and mix well.

In another bowl, beat the 3 egg whites until soft peaks form. Add remaining 2 tablespoons of sugar and whisk for a few more seconds. Gently fold whites into cheese mixture. Fill ramekins two-thirds full and place in large roasting pan. Carefully pour enough very hot water into the roasting pan to reach halfway up the sides of the ramekins. Bake for 15 minutes, remove from oven, and allow to cool completely. Run a warm knife along the edge of the ramekins to loosen the edges. Lay a plate over top of the ramekin and invert to gently unmould soufflé.

Meanwhile, plunge peaches into boiling water for 10 seconds and peel away the skins. Halve each peach, removing and discarding pits. Simmer peach halves in skillet with Icewine, sugar, vanilla bean (scraping seeds into pan), cinnamon, cloves, and lemon juice for 20 minutes. Remove and discard vanilla bean, cinnamon, and cloves. When peaches are cool enough to handle, purée them and the poaching liquid. Chill for an hour.

Serve soufflés topped with peach slice, lime zest, and peach purée.

Serve with chilled Vidal or Sparkling Icewine.

Vanilla-Scented Pound Cake with Buttered Almonds

MAKES ONE 9-INCH CAKE

Oak-aged Icewine's vanilla, toasty flavours and elegant body make it an ideal wine for this simple yet elegant dessert.

Recipe by Inniskillin Resident Chef
Izabela Kalabis-Sacco

CAKE
¾ cup (180 mL) unsalted butter, room temperature

¾ cup (180 mL) sugar

3 eggs, separated

1 vanilla bean, split lengthwise

pinch of salt

1 ⅓ cups (330 mL) all-purpose flour, sifted

BUTTERED ALMONDS
3 Tbsp (45 mL) unsalted butter

3 Tbsp (45 mL) sugar

⅓ cup (80 mL) whole unsalted almonds

2 Tbsp (30 mL) heavy cream

Preheat oven to 350°F (180°C). Butter a 9-inch (22 cm) loaf pan and line with parchment paper.

Using an electric mixer, cream butter and sugar until light and fluffy. Add the egg yolks one by one, beating and scraping down mixture after each addition. Using a small knife, scrape the seeds from the vanilla bean and add to the mixture.

In another bowl, beat egg whites with a pinch of salt until firm peaks appear. Alternating with the flour, add the egg whites to the butter mixture until well incorporated. Spoon into prepared loaf pan and bake for 30 to 35 minutes or until top springs back when lightly touched. Turn out onto a rack immediately to cool.

Meanwhile, melt butter and sugar in a saucepan. When sugar has dissolved add almonds. Stir mixture over medium heat until it turns a light caramel colour, about 6 to 7 minutes. Add cream and stir for a minute until liquid is smooth. Remove from heat and pour over pound cake.

Serve with chilled Oak-aged Vidal Icewine.

ICEWINE WITH FOOD 173

APPENDICES

Endnotes

ART

1 Canadian Vintners Association, media release, Paris, France, 23rd June, 2000.

2 Peter Steponkus, Role of plasma membrane in freezing injury and acclimation, Cornell University.

3 Charles Guy, from Genetics of Freezing Tolerance, University of Florida.

4 Duman, chair of Notre Dame's Department of Biological Sciences.

5 John Carey, Crystalizing the Truth, National Wildlife, Dec./Jan. 1985, pp. 43–44.

6 Judi Manning.

SCIENCE

1 Data was acquired from Dr. Sandra Yee, Brock University, using the Niagara Agricultural Weather News (NAWN).

2 D.L. Inglis, G. Pigeau, J. Quai, M. Pistor, and K. Kaiser. Cool Climate Oenology and Viticulture Institute, Brock University, 500 Glenridge Avenue, St. Catharines, ON, Canada L2S 3A1 [dinglis@brocku.ca].

3 Gary Pigeau and Debra Inglis, Upregulation of ALD3 and GPD1 in Saccharomyces cerevisiae during Icewine fermentation. Journal of Applied Microbiology, 99: 112–125, 2005

4 Derek Kontkanen, Debra Inglis, Gary Pickering, and Andrew Reynolds, The effect of yeast inoculation rate, acclimatization and nutrient addition on Icewine fermentation. American Journal of Enology and Viticulture, 66:363–370, 2004.

5 Gary Pigeau and Debra Inglis, Upregulation of ALD3 and GPD1 in Saccharomyces cerevisiae during Icewine fermentation. Journal of Applied Microbiology, 99: 112–125, 2005.

6 Klaus Sutterlin, Petra Hoffmann-Boller und Jurg Gafner, Eidgenossische Forschungsanstalt Wadenswil, Switzerland in the Schweiz Z. Obst-Weinbau, Nov. 24/03.

7 R.E. Subben, J.I. Husnik, R. VanTwest, G. van der Merwe, H.J.J. van Vuuren, "Autochthonous microbial population in a Niagara Peninsula Icewine must, Food Research International 2003."

8 Nurgel, C.; Inglis, D.; Pickering, G.J.; Reynolds, A.; Brindle, I., Population Changes of Yeast Flora Associated with Vidal and Riesling Icewine Grapes—Across Four Successive Harvest Dates.

9 Dr. Canan Nurgel, Dr. Debra Inglis, Dr. Gary Pickering, Dr. Andrew Reynolds, Dr. Ian Brindle, CCOVI, Brock University, St. Catharines, Ontario, "Dynamics of Indigenous and Inoculated Yeast Populations in Vidal and Riesling Icewine." American Journal of Enology and Viticulture, 2004.

10 Canan Nurgel, Gary J. Pickering, and Debra L. Inglis, Sensory and chemical characteristics of Canadian Icewines. Journal of the Science of Food and Agriculture, 84: 1675–1684, 2004.

TASTE

1 Linda M. Bartoshuk, Yale University School of Medicine, Department of Surgery.

2 Dr Isabelle Lesschauvre, Director, CCOVI, Brock University.

Tables

INNISKILLIN ICEWINE HISTORY—VIDAL GRAPES AND ONTARIO HARVESTS UNLESS OTHERWISE STATED

Vintage	Harvest Date	Harvest Temp.	Harvest Brix	Total Acid Grams per Litre at Harvest	Alcohol %	Res. Sugar
1983 Vidal	Eaten by birds					
1984 Vidal	Jan. 8, 1985	-15°				
1985 Vidal	Dec. 15, 1985	-13°				
1986 Vidal	Jan. 23, 1987	-17°	55.0° Brix	13.4 g/l	10.0%	180 g/l
1987 Vidal	Jan. 05, 1988	-15°	45.0° Brix	12.9 g/l	11.1%	164 g/l
1988 Vidal	Feb. 7–8, 1989	-10°	38.0° Brix	11.0 g/l	11.5%	149 g/l
1989 Vidal	Dec. 4, 7, 8, 14, 15, 1989	-12°	38.9° Brix	13.0 g/l	11.1%	148 g/l
1990 Vidal	Jan. 4, 8, 1991	-13°	44.0° Brix	11.6 g/l	11.7%	129 g/l
1991 Vidal	Jan. 5, 8, 1992	-16°	37.3° Brix	9.8 g/l	11.0%	135 g/l
1992 Vidal	Dec. 26, 1992	-13°	38.0° Brix	11.5 g/l	11.1%	145 g/l
1993 Vidal	Dec. 26, 31, 1993	-17°	41.0° Brix	11.5 g/l	12.1%	155 g/l
1994 Vidal	Dec. 13,14, 1994	N.A.	38.0° Brix	11.5 g/l	10.5%	151 g/l
1995 Vidal	Dec. 12,13, 1995	N.A.	42.0° Brix	12.1 g/l	11.0%	185 g/l
1996 Vidal	Dec. 20, 31, 1996/Jan. 1, 11, 12, 16–19, 1997	N.A.	38.35° Brix	12.5 g/l	10.5%	192 g/l
1997 Vidal	Dec. 31, 1997; Feb. 15, 1998	-11°	40.0° Brix	12.0 g/l	10.5%	225 g/l
1998 Vidal	Jan. 1–12, 1999	-13°	43.0° Brix	13.1 g/l	9.0%	270 g/l
1999 Vidal	Jan. 26, 2000	-11°	42.4° Brix	12.1 g/l	10.5%	247 g/l
2000 Vidal	Dec. 20, 2000; Jan. 9, 2001	-11°	40.3° Brix	12.2 g/l	9.5%	232 g/l
2001 Vidal	Dec. 27, 2001; Feb. 4, 5, 28; Mar. 4, 5, 2002	-12°	36.8° Brix	10.9 g/l	10.5%	209 g/l
2002 Vidal	Dec. 2–5, 8–11,16–18, 2001; Jan. 7, 21, 2003	-11°	38.2° Brix	11.9 g/l	9.9%	212 g/l
2003 Vidal	Jan. 6–31, 2004	-11°	39.8° Brix	12.0 g/l	10.5%	222 g/l
2004 Vidal	Dec. 19, 20, 28, 2004; Jan. 17–21, 2005	-17°	39.0° Brix	13.5 g/l	10.8%	195 g/l
2005 Vidal	Dec. 13, 14, 21, 2005; Jan. 15–16, 2006	-9.5°	380.0° Brix	10.5 g/l	10.6%	192 g/l
2006 Vidal	Jan. 16, 21, 28, & 31, 2007	-10°	38.8° Brix	8.0 g/l	9.4%	210 g/l
1997 Riesling	Dec.30, 1997	-9°	40.0° Brix	10.2 g/l	10.5%	199 g/l
1998 Riesling	Dec. 23, 1998	-10°	43.3° Brix	12.0 g/l	9.5%	224 g/l
1999 Riesling	Dec. 30, 1999; Jan. 1, 2000	-10°	39.4° Brix	10.5 g/l	10.5%	200 g/l
2001 Riesling	Feb. 4, 5, 6, 2002; Mar. 5, 2002	-9°	37.5° Brix	10.3 g/l	9.5%	214 g/l
2002 Riesling	Dec. 3, 4, 5, 6, 9, 17, 18, 2002; Jan. 7, 16, 17, 2003	-9°	37.9° Brix	11.0 g/l	10.0%	225 g/l
2003 Riesling	Jan. 6–31, 2004	-10°	38.8° Brix	10.0 g/l	11.0%	225 g/l
2004 Riesling	Dec. 19, 20, 28, 2004; Jan. 17–21, 2005	-10°	38.2° Brix	12.6 g/l	10.8%	183 g/l
2005 Riesling	Dec. 13, 14, 21, 2005; Jan. 15–16, 2006	-10°	38.0° Brix	10.0 g/l	9.5%	185 g/l
2006 Riesling	Jan. 16, 21, 28, 31, 2007	-10°	38.0° Brix	10.0 g/l	9.5%	220 g/l
1995 Cabernet Franc	Dec. 12, 1995	-10°	42.0° Brix	11.1 g/l	11.0%	195 g/l
1997 Cabernet Franc	Dec. 31, 1997	-12°	40.0° Brix	10.3 g/l	10.5%	213 g/l
1998 Cabernet Franc	Dec. 29, 1998	-12°	45.7° Brix	11.8 g/l	10.0%	260 g/l
1999 Cabernet Franc	Jan. 3–19, 2000	-9°	42.2 ° Brix		10.0%	20.9 g/l
2001 Cabernet Franc	Jan. 3, 2001; Feb. 4, 5, 11, 2002	-14°	38.8° Brix	8.9 g/l	10.0%	200 g/l
2002 Cabernet Franc	Dec. 2, 3, 4, 9, 2002; Jan. 7, 16, 17, 21, 2003	-12°	39.5° Brix	11.3 g/l	10.0%	210 g/l
2003 Cabernet Franc	Jan. 6, 7, 8, 2004	-12°	40.5° Brix	10.8 g/l	10.0%	190 g/l
2004 Cabernet Franc	Dec. 19, 20, 28, 2004; Jan. 17–21, 2005	-12°	39.5° Brix	7.3 g/l	10.9%	195 g/l
2005 Cabernet Franc	Dec. 13, 14, 21, 2005 & Jan. 15–16, 2006	-11°	42.0° Brix	10.5 g/l	10.6%	192 g/l
2006 Cabernet Franc	Jan. 16, 21, 28, 31, 2007	-12°	38.0° Brix	7.2 g/l	9.4%	210 g/l

NUMBER OF ICEWINE HOURS AT -8, -9, -10, -11, -12, -13°C AS RECORDED DURING THE WINTER MONTHS OF DEC '01, JAN '02, AND FEB '02 (UP TO AND INCLUDING FEB 17) FOR THE NIAGARA PENINSULA, ON.

All data was acquired from Dr. Sandra Yee, Brock University, and the Niagara Agricultural Weather News (NAWN).

Location	Month	-8 °C 36.16 Brix	-9°C 36.16 Brix	-10 °C 36.16 Brix	-11 °C 36.16 Brix	-12°C 36.16 Brix	-13 °C 36.16 Brix
Niagara Parkway Niagara-on-the-Lake	Dec.'01	2.5	0.7	0.0	0.0	0.0	0.0
	Jan.'02	6.4	0.0	0.0	0.0	0.0	0.0
	Feb.'02	31.7	15.2	3.0	3.0	2.2	0.2
	Total	40.6	15.9	3.0	3.0	2.2	0.2
Niagara College Niagara-on-the-Lake	Dec.'01	2.0	0.0	0.0	0.0	0.0	0.0
	Jan.'02	5.6	0.0	0.0	0.0	0.0	0.0
	Feb.'02	35.0	17.3	10.5	3.8	2.8	0.5
	Total	42.6	17.3	10.5	3.8	2.8	0.5
Lakeshore Niagara-on-the-Lake	Dec.'01	8.2	2.3	0.0	0.0	0.0	0.0
	Jan.'02	6.4	0.0	0.0	0.0	0.0	0.0
	Feb.'02	31.5	14.0	5.7	2.0	1.3	0.0
	Total	46.1	16.3	5.7	2.0	1.3	0.0
West St. Catharines and Pelham	Dec.'01	11.3	2.4	1.3	0.6	0.0	0.0
	Jan.'02	27.5	11.0	2.2	0.0	0.0	0.0
	Feb.'02	36.5	20.0	13.3	5.7	4.4	3.3
	Total	75.3	33.4	16.8	6.3	4.4	3.3
Highway 8 Jordan	Dec.'01	4.8	2.0	0.1	0.0	0.0	0.0
	Jan.'02	18.7	3.1	0.0	0.0	0.0	0.0
	Feb.'02	33	19.6	9.0	5.3	2.6	0.0
	Total	56.5	24.7	9.1	5.3	2.6	0.0

ICEWINE—BRITISH COLUMBIA 2000–2004

The data was received from the B.C. Wine Institute, 1737 Pandosy Street, Kelowna, B.C. V1Y 1R2. All data was compiled by Karl J. Kaiser, July 2005.

	2000	2001	2002	2003	2004	5 year total	5 year average
Approximate acres reported:	118.78	127.61	153.00	655.00	158.51	754.88	150.98
Approximate tons estimated in Oct.:	592.00	570.50	655.00	808.15	732.00	3,357.15	671.43
Approximate tons picked:	554.55	343.50	160.00	528.00	510.00	2,096.05	419.21
Approximate volume of processed juice (L):	116,200	62,200	41,800	106,060	105,000	431,260	86,252
Equals metric tonnes estimated in Oct.:	537.06	517.56	594.12	733.15	664.04	3,046.03	721.84
Equals metric tonnes picked:	503.08	311.62	145.15	479.00	462.67	1,901.52	380.30
Litres per tonne based on actual tonnage picked†:	280.98	199.60	287.98	221.42	226.96	1,166.94	233.39
Litres per tonne based on estimate†† (juice yield):	216.36	120.18	70.34	144.66	158.12	709.66	141.93

† 23.3% yield. Approx. 23–25% yield based on actual tonnage harvested.
†† 14.2% yield. Approx. 14% yield based on October estimates.

ICEWINE—ONTARIO, 1997–2004

The following data is recorded in litres, and separated by vintage and grape variety. From 1997–1999, production breakdown by variety was not available. The data was received from VQA for 1997–1999 and from VQAO from 2000–2004.

All data was compiled by Karl J. Kaiser, July 2005. Tonnes were based on netted tonnes recorded in October.

Year	Vidal	Riesling	Cabernet Franc	Gewürz-traminer	Cabernet Sauvignon	Chardonnay	Others	Total Litres	Total Tonnes	Litres/Tonnes Juice yield
1997 (El Niño)	n/a	n/a	n/a	n/a	n/a	n/a	n/a	263,000	2,916	90.2
1998	n/a	n/a	n/a	n/a	n/a	n/a	n/a	609,000	2,658	229.1
1999	n/a	n/a	n/a	n/a	n/a	n/a	n/a	304,000	1,975	153.9
2000	261,007	50,882	9,819	5,355	220	200	1,250	328,686	2,335	138.3
2001 (El Niño)	307,199	29,128	22,497	3,056	-0-	2,450	395	366,728	3,176	114.8
2002	401,772	128,533	72,221	11,010	6,885	1,000	3,710	625,131	4,089	152.9
2003	371,578	44,630	16,163	1,200	1,200	400	2,500	437,671	3,372	129.8
2004	688,966	102,794	89,480	6,110	5,275	3,720	3,825	900,170	5,808	155.0
5 Year Total	2,030,522	355,967	210,180	26,731	13,580	7,770	11,635	2,658,386	18,780	690.8
5 Year Average	406,104	71,193	42,036	5,346	2,716	1,154	2,327	531,677	3,756	138.1

Percent of total Icewine by variety

	Vidal	Riesling	Cabernet Franc	Gewürz-traminer	Cabernet Sauvignon	Chardonnay	Others	Total
	76.38%	13.39%	7.91%	1.00%	0.51%	0.29%	0.44%	100%

ICEWINE—EUROPE 2000-2004

Summary of Icewine volumes from Germany, Austria, and Canada (British Columbia and Ontario) over the last five years. The volumes from Germany and Austria were reported as finished wines which already have passed the "quality wine" test and tasting offices. Ontario and British Columbia volumes were reported as juice volumes (prior to fermentation) which are shown in brackets. A 12.0% deduction (correction) was made to account for losses through subsequent juice settling, fermentation, and filtration losses in Ontario's and British Columbia's Icewine volumes.

	2000	2001	2002	2003	2004	5 year total	5 year average
GERMANY							
Ahr	21	6	7	10	1	45	9
Mittelrhein	18	11	29	57	15	130	26
Mosel-Saar-Ruwer	573	391	623	982	326	2,895	579
Nahe	241	131	225	562	201	1,360	272
Rheinhessen	2,453	1,577	2,533	7,801	7,816	22,180	4,436
Pfalz	1,369	614	1,299	2,049	1,941	7,272	1,454
Rheingau	84	50	121	252	66	573	115
Hess. Bergstrasse	143	72	151	265	99	730	146
Franken	200	56	67	137	154	614	123
Württemberg	256	86	164	95	67	905	181
Baden	307	84	293	113	108	905	181
Saale-Unstrut	3	10	3	15	8	39	8
Sachsen	2	1	2	14	20	39	8
Germany Total Litres	567,000	308,900	551,700	1,235,200	1,082,200	3,745,000	749,000
Austria Total Litres	230,400	100,300	133,700	115,960	157,710	738,070	147,614
Combined Total Litres	797,400	409,200	685,400	1,351,160	1,239,910	4,483,070	896,614
Ontario Total Litres	289,243	322,721	550,115	385,151	792,150	2,339,380	467,876
B.C. Total Litres	102,256	55,358	36,784	93,333	92,400	382,149	76,430
Canada Total Litres	391,500	377,457	586,899	478,483	884,550	2,718,888	543,778

From the above table we can calculate that over the last five (5) years, Germany and Austria combined produced 1.65 times as much Icewine as British Columbia and Ontario combined. Germany alone produced approximately 1.4 litres more than Canada, and still ranks as the largest Icewine producer in the world, which also amounts to 5.1 times that of Austria. Canada on the other hand, produces about 3.7 times as much as Austria and Ontario produced about 6.1 times as much as B.C. in the last 5-year period as an average/per year, which is 86% in Ontario and 14.0% in B.C.

ICEWINE COMPOSITION

Compositional Analysis of 345 Icewine juices from the 2003 and 2004 vintages in the Niagara Peninsula, ON. Samples were collected by Gerald Klose, Inniskillin Wines, with testing and data compiled by Dr. Debra Inglis, Gary Pigeau, Derek Kontkanen, Jamie Quai, and Marc Pistor, CCOVI, Brock University, and Karl Kaiser and Gerald Klose, Inniskillin Wines.

Variety	Soluble Solids (°Brix)	Amino Acid Nitrogen (g/L)	Ammonia Nitrogen (g/L)	Total Yeast Assimilable Nitrogen (g/L)	pH	Titratable Acidity (g/L tartaric acid)	Malic Acid (g/L)	%TA as Malic Acid
Riesling	38.0 ± 2.1	381.7 ± 132.6	79.7 ± 38.6	461.3 ± 166.5	3.22 ± 0.18	9.0 ± 1.7	5.39 ± 1.17	67.0 ± 7.5
Vidal	39.3 ± 1.7	497.7 ± 105.2	57.3 ± 18.7	555.0 ± 120.2	3.38 ± 0.16	10.5 ± 1.5	7.8 ± 1.3	84.0 ± 10.5
Cabernet Franc	39.4 ± 2.0	292.9 ± 116.7	22.3 ± 8.5	315.3 ± 123.0	3.79 ± 0.24	5.7 ± 1.2	4.68 ± 0.83	93.1 ± 12.4

MEAN TEMPERATURES OVER 78 YEARS IN THE
NIAGARA PENINSULA, ON, AND THE OKANAGAN VALLEY, BC.

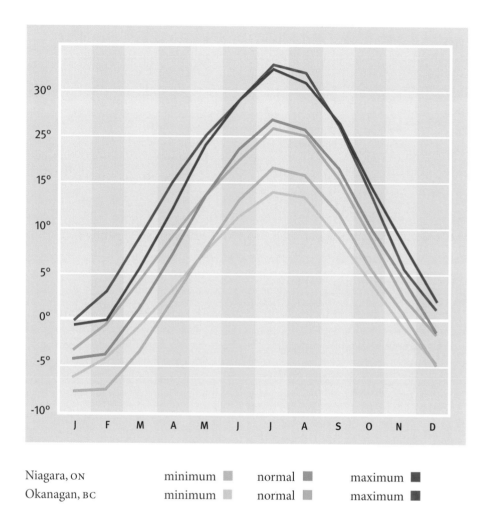

| Niagara, ON | minimum ▦ | normal ▦ | maximum ■ |
| Okanagan, BC | minimum ▦ | normal ▦ | maximum ■ |

Mean temperature values were calculated for the past 78 years and plotted as a function of the month of the year. The temperatures at the Niagara District Airport in the Niagara Peninsula were acquired from the Niagara District Weather Office, Environment Canada, and the temperatures at the Summerland Research Station in the Okanagan were acquired from the Summerland Station, Agriculture Canada. Minimum temperatures (> minimum Ontario, (minimum Okanagan) were computed from the average daily minimum temperatures for the month. Maximum temperatures (! maximum Ontario, "maximum Okanagan) were computed from the average daily maximum temperatures for the month. The normal temperatures ('normal Ontario, (normal Okanagan) were computed averages over 78 years between the daily maximum and daily minimum temperatures.

Credits

Index

RECIPE INDEX

Acknowledgements

Karl and I wanted to especially thank a number of creative people who assisted in various components in the book.

Georg Riedel and his staff. The entire Inniskillin team.

Maximillian Kaiser who spent hours in front of his computer at his company Spiral Graphis, for his patience and creative composition in collecting much of the material and assisting with the composition of the original draft.

Debi Pratt who was always available to provide a critical eye to details of the book.

Shari Darling who worked on the original concept for food and wine and for creating the very functional Icewine flavour wheel.

Food writer Lynn Ogryzlo who, along with photographer Stephen Dominique, created a beautiful exhibition of food and wine that was such a gift to us from our beloved Izabela Kalabis-Sacco.

Roger Provost for his passion and commitment to building a luxury global brand.

The team at Key Porter, Jordan Fenn, Michael Mouland, and Martin Gould for their support and guidance.

Dr. Isabelle Leschaeve, Dr. Debra Inglis, and Dr. Gary Pickering at ccovi for their knowledge and expertise.

A special thank you to our wives, Sylvia Kaiser and Anna Netter-Ziraldo, for their input and support.

Dawn Grundy for her adminstrative and personal support.

Many others such as Alexandra Risen; Ferran Adrià, El Bulli, Spain; Rod Pasic; Ed Ayoub; Dr. Uwe Kils; Tracey Butler; Kathryn Korchuck; George Soleas; Tracey Butler; J.R. Patterson; Helen Fischer; Leona Gilbert; Kevin Karl; Vincor Sales and Marketing; and Catherine Didulka and her Vincor creative team.

Postscript

On July 31, 1975, Inniskillin Wines incorporated, and its founders Karl J. Kaiser and Donald J.P. Ziraldo were granted the first winery licence in Ontario, Canada, since 1929.

Established in Niagara-on-the-Lake, Inniskillin was founded upon and dedicated to the principle of producing and bottling outstanding wines from select wine grapes grown in the Niagara Peninsula.

In 1971, Ziraldo received a degree in Agriculture from the University of Guelph, after which he operated a family nursery specializing in fruit trees and grapevines. Karl, a native of Austria, had moved to Canada after meeting and marrying his Canadian wife, Silvia. He had a degree in Chemistry from Brock University and had begun experimenting with home winemaking.

One fateful day, Karl bought some French hybrid grapevines from Donald at the nursery and, some time afterward, they shared a bottle of Karl's homemade wine. After a lot of dreaming and talking, they decided to apply for a wine licence. None had been issued since 1929.

The late General George Kitching, Chairman of the Liquor Control Board of Ontario, shared their vision of a premium estate winery producing varietal wines from grapes grown in the Niagara Peninsula.

In 1991 Inniskillin was awarded the prestigious Grand Prix d'Honneur at Vin-Expo, in Bordeaux France for the 1989 Icewine. The rest is history!

The name Inniskillin is Irish and derived from the famous Irish regiment, the Inniskilling Fusiliers. Colonel Cooper, a member of this regiment, served in North America in the War of 1812. Upon completion of his military service, he was granted Crown land that he named the Inniskillin Farm.

Author Biographies

KARL J. KAISER, co-founder of Inniskillin Wines, went for some years to school in a private monastery school in Austria where viticulture and winemaking were a time-honored tradition. Kaiser came to Canada in 1969 after marrying Sylvia, a Canadian residing temporarily in Austria. Their family grew with the addition of three children, Magda, Andrea, and Max, and now seven grandchildren. For winemaker Kaiser, following his heart led to his destiny as one of the premier practitioners of the art of making Icewine. Karl's hands-on learning in Austria melded with a biochemistry degree from Canada's Brock University. His extensive research in both Old and New World Icewine vinification throughout years gave him the impetus to create Inniskillin's unique style of Icewine. His efforts paid off early when he won the highest accolade at France's prestigious VinExpo in 1991, the Grand Prix d'Honneur, for his 1989 Vidal Icewine. Over the years many awards, tributes, and commendations have been given to Kaiser. He received The Order of Ontario and an Honorary Doctorate from Brock University. He realized that the life of an Icewine maker is in the hands of Mother Nature, a reality to which Kaiser pays great respect.

DONALD J.P. ZIRALDO was born in Niagara, Canada, the son of Italian immigrants from Friuli, Italy. Co-founder of Inniskillin wines, he is an educator, creative entrepreneur, and founding chairman of the Vintners Quality Alliance (VQA).

Ziraldo has served on numerous Boards and charities, was awarded the Order of Canada and named one of Canada's Top 25 CEOs of the Century by *National Post* magazine. He has received several degrees, including an Honorary Doctorate (LLD) from Brock University. Ziraldo is an extreme skier and collector of Art Deco.

www.ziraldo.ca

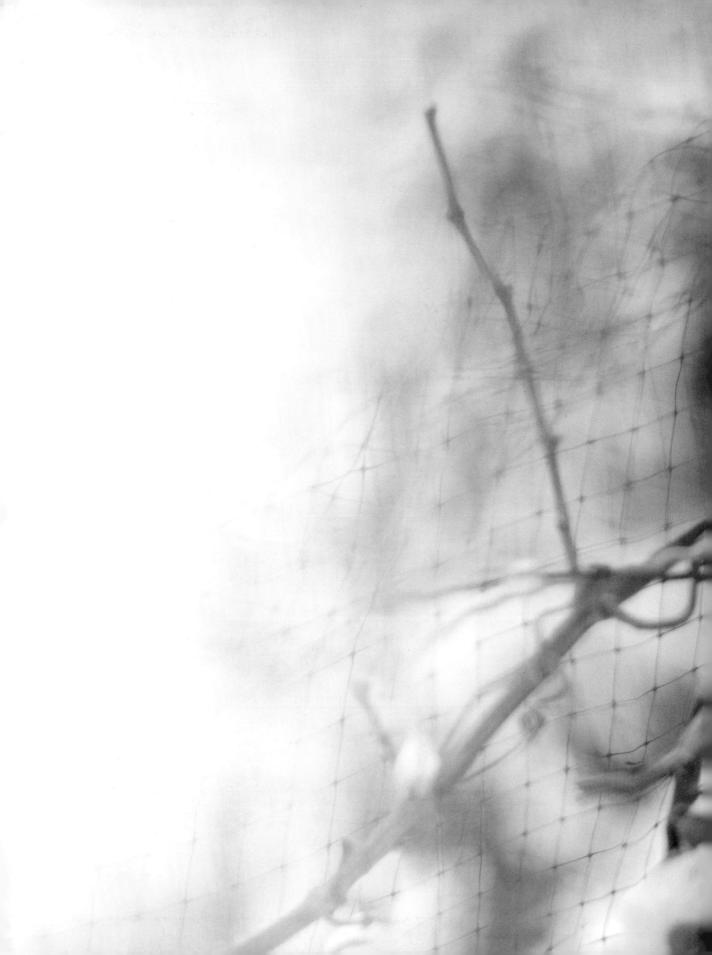